10 Things You *Aren't* Telling Him

JULIE **CLINTON**

HARVEST HOUSE PUBLISHERS

EUGENE, OREGON

Cover by Koechel Peterson & Associates, Inc., Minneapolis, Minnesota

Cover photo © Amanda Rohde / iStockphoto

This book contains stories in which the author has changed people's names and some details of their situations to protect their privacy.

10 THINGS YOU AREN'T TELLING HIM
Copyright © 2009 by Julie Clinton
Published by Harvest House Publishers
Eugene, Oregon 97402
www.harvesthousepublishers.com

Library of Congress Cataloging-in-Publication Data

Clinton, Julie
10 things you aren't telling him / Julie Clinton.
    p. cm.
ISBN 978-0-7369-2111-4 (pbk.)
1. Marriage—Religious aspects—Christianity. 2. Women—Psychology. I.Title. II. Title: Ten things you aren't telling him.
BV835.C577 2009
248.8'435—dc22
                                                           2009009303

Printed in the United States of America

09 10 11 12 13 14 15 16 / VP-NI / 10 9 8 7 6 5 4 3 2 1

*This book is dedicated to
the love of my life—my husband, Tim.
I am blessed by your unconditional
love, safety, and openness.
Thank you for dreaming.*

Acknowledgments

I am a little pencil in the hand of a writing God
who is sending a love letter to the world.

Mother Teresa

I love this quote because it reminds me of the incredible team of little pencils at Extraordinary Women—a team that works tirelessly to deliver God's love letter to the world. Because of His love and grace, I owe my deepest thanks first and foremost to the true Lover of my soul—Jesus Christ.

A special thank you to Pat Springle for teaming up with me on this book. Pat, your wisdom and gift of writing are beautifully used for God's glory. Thank you for your hard work and dedication to the Word of God.

Kudos to Harvest House Publishers for their support and dedication. In particular to Terry Glaspey, Carolyn McCready, and Gene Skinner for providing a special platform to reach women all across America.

To Joshua Straub, who takes the lead on so many of our projects as a liaison, writer, researcher, and editor. And to Amy Feigel and Laura Faidley for their editing, research, and insight—you guys are great!

To the hardworking Extraordinary Women team, thank you for the long hours during the week and dedication to weekends spent on the road to serve Christ and women across this nation. I love working with you all!

Mom, I wouldn't be where I am today without your faithful prayers for me. You have given me a beautiful example of what it means to be a wife, mother, and woman of God.

And to my husband, Tim. I can only write a book on this topic because of your unconditional love, grace, and passion for our marriage to become better than I would have ever dreamed possible. Megan and Zach, you color my world with rainbows of joy. I am so blessed by the love you bring to my heart. The best is yet to be!

Contents

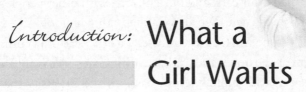

Introduction: What a Girl Wants

*The great question that has never been answered,
and which I have not yet been able to answer,
despite my thirty years of research into the feminine
soul, is "What does a woman want?"*

SIGMUND FREUD

SOMETIMES, A GIRL JUST WANTS HER MAN TO UNDERSTAND HER.
My marriage, early on, was difficult. Very difficult. After several
days of fighting, my husband, Tim, and I were both exhausted. He
wanted to fix it; I wanted him to understand me. Money was a problem.
So what did he do? He came home with a bouquet of flowers. When
you're fighting over money and your man spends $50 on a bouquet
of flowers—well, needless to say, they were not what I wanted, and
they weren't going to pay next month's rent either! Tim, noticing my
utter disappointment, quickly became agitated, turned around, and
chucked the flowers on the floor—hard! I cried, privately wondering
if this was what I signed up for.

When life gets tough, other voices might tell us the grass is greener
and we deserve more. We often compare ourselves to other people, and

even though we want to be thankful for what we have, our desires for something bigger and better are never far away. The problem is that we usually compare ourselves and our situation with the very best of what we see on television, in advertisements, and around town. We compare our figures with the models in the *Sports Illustrated Swimsuit Issue* and our hair with the silky-haired girls on shampoo commercials. We compare our houses, our kitchens, our cars, and our children with other people's.

And it doesn't end there. We also want a man who looks like Brad Pitt. We want him be as sensuous and sexy as the lead in a romance novel, as patient as the pope, and as rich as Bill Gates. We want a man who will look at us with more interest, passion, and intensity than he gives to the Super Bowl. We want a man who is totally, completely, unreservedly into us!

With that as our standard, no wonder we're often disappointed when our guys are standing in front of our refrigerators and scratching themselves. Of course, we've made our choice, and we're committed to stay with them, but many of us can't get past that nagging sense that it could be better than this—it should be better than this. Look at this quote by Judith Viorst I found from the 1970s:

> Infatuation is when you think he's as sexy as Robert Redford, as smart as Henry Kissinger, as noble as Ralph Nader, as funny as Woody Allen, and as athletic as Jimmy Connors. Love is when you realize that he's as sexy as Woody Allen, as smart as Jimmy Connors, as funny as Ralph Nader, as athletic as Henry Kissinger, and nothing like Robert Redford—but you'll take him anyway.

A Sacred Romance

I want to explain something at the outset. From what the Bible tells us, life is all about relationships—particularly with God and with those we love, and especially with our husbands. You don't have to go very far in the Bible to see that God desires a relationship with each and every one of us. Even more, He is a pursuer God, and He works to win our hearts. His desire is for us. When His love touches us, everything changes.

Go back with me for a moment to the book of Genesis. We see that God placed the same relational impetus He has for us into the hearts of both men and women. After God completed the rest of creation, and before sin, sickness, death, heartache, and pain entered the world, He looked around the Garden and realized something wasn't good (Genesis 2:18). Even though God walked with Adam in perfect harmony, He knew that it was not good for man to be alone. So what did He do? He created us! Women! That's right, out of the rib of Adam He created an *ezer,* a suitable helper, to come alongside and complement Adam. Bone of his bone and flesh of his flesh. God gave him Eve. He designed the two for the deepest of all intimacy—united as one flesh. An intimacy bathed in beauty, innocence, and freedom. They were naked together and unashamed. There for one another. Safe.

But anything that has that much potential for good has that much potential for hurt and pain as well. You don't have to read very far into the next chapter of Genesis to find that all hell is against anything God wants to bless. When Tim speaks to groups, he usually starts with this phrase: "We are broken in relationship, but we're also healed in relationship."

What's Going On: Three Reasons We're Not Communicating

As I travel to Extraordinary Women conferences and meet thousands of ladies across the country, I hear stories of relational tension. Nearly every woman I have met who lives in America has experienced it. The hectic pace, enormous pressure, and intense (but often hidden) pain in a woman's world puts undeserved stress on her most cherished relationship. In fact, Dr. Richard Swenson wrote in his book *Margin* that most couples spend as little as four minutes a day in meaningful interaction. Stop a minute. Think about that. Only four minutes of quality relationship time—sitting, listening, holding hands, rubbing his shoulders…just being together. The result is that we feel empty and exhausted, yet we're yearning to be heard and loved!

Forgetting the Simple Things

> The best things in life are nearest: Breath in your nostrils, light in your eyes, flowers at your feet, duties at your hand, the path of right just before you. Then do not grasp at the stars, but do life's plain, common work as it comes, certain that daily duties and daily bread are the sweetest things in life.
>
> ROBERT LOUIS STEVENSON

Every summer our family takes a vacation trip to Myrtle Beach. And every summer leading up to the trip, Tim and I vow to leave the kids with my parents one night and go on a date. But year after year, for whatever reason, we couldn't make it happen. Time just seemed to run out on us. So you can imagine my excitement the year we actually figured out a way to make our date-night dream come true.

After coming in from the beach, kicking off my sandals, showering, putting on makeup, forcing my hair into place in the humid air, and getting dolled up in the finest outfit my summer beach vacation suitcase had to offer, I was ready. When I finally stepped out into the living area to meet Tim, I was one big smile from ear to ear. Tim gently kissed my lips, I took his hand, and out the door we went.

As we drove around looking for a restaurant, seconds turned into minutes, and minutes turned into hours. I was starving, and so was he. The traffic at the beach and my now-flat hair didn't help. The only suitable restaurant we could find was booked full for the evening. Our dream date gradually turned into a disaster filled with sarcasm, nit-picking, and finding all of each other's faults. With empty stomachs and agitated attitudes, we resigned ourselves to wandering around a resort called Barefoot Landing. We quietly walked together, all dressed up with nowhere to go but for a stroll on a boardwalk.

And then something happened. We took a breath and simply started talking like adults to each other. Heckling eventually turned into hugging and holding each other over the moonlit lake.

Obviously, our irritation had nothing to do with each other. We were simply disappointed. We were frustrated about our evening, and then we became frustrated that we were frustrated. Couples create a lot of the trouble for themselves by digging in their heels and fighting over things that they can't explain or that don't matter. That bickering takes the place of honest communication. A lot of these couples could resolve most of their differences if they would simply, calmly, and honestly talk.

Sick as Our Secrets

The pace of our days and our crazy schedules can knock the romance out of our relationships. And most of us live with various pressures, so we experience an abundance of anger and tension. We nag, criticize, badger, and yell. Our talk breaks down even more, or we give up talking altogether. But one thing is sure—and the best way to say this is with a double negative—you cannot *not* communicate. You're constantly sending messages—positive or negative, verbal or nonverbal.

The truth is that we are as sick as our secrets and the things we hold inside. Many women have poured out their hearts to me about sexual abuse, affairs, checkbook problems, abortions, addiction, eating disorders...but when I asked if they'd talked to their husbands or boyfriends about these things, they looked horrified. "Are you kidding? I'd never tell him about that!" This secret world is a perfect breeding ground for shame, and shame infects every aspect of our lives. It ruins our sense of confidence, causes us to be on edge instead of relaxed, and forces us to defend ourselves even when no enemy is around.

Of course, I'm not advocating that we walk in the door tonight, spill our guts to our men, and see what happens. We need to be wise about how and when we begin to tell the secrets we've buried for so long. But we need to start the process of uncovering them, talking about them with a trusted friend, and then judiciously sharing them with the men in our lives.

You might wonder, *But aren't those things in the past?* Well, your past isn't your past if it is still affecting your present. I've known women who found the courage and tact to speak up about things that have haunted them for decades. The process was difficult, but it almost always led to incredible freedom. The secrets had created barriers between them and their husbands, and when those barriers were removed, the couples enjoyed richer, deeper, and more loving relationships than they'd ever dreamed possible.

Time to Talk

Without a doubt, you long to love and be loved passionately, exclusively, and unreservedly. But when you don't talk with your man about something that matters in your life, he eventually notices. You may talk to your friends about it, but that keeps him from knowing the longings in your heart and leads him to believe your friends are more important to you than he is. Or you may hide it and end up angry at him because you don't feel the way you're supposed to. Either way, this effort to protect yourself from

> To effectively communicate, we must realize that we are all different in the way we perceive the world and use this understanding as a guide to our communication with others.
>
> ANTHONY ROBBINS

added hurt and pressure usually pushes him further away. He feels disrespected. And the subtle and not-so-subtle ways you might drop hints about the things you think he should already know—the things that really matter to you—actually cut him off. He doesn't understand what you want, you don't understand why he's distant, and love fades.

Please understand—this is more than just a communication problem. Virtually all couples are occasionally too busy to talk about important things. That's natural. But when not communicating becomes the norm, something deeper goes amiss. We no longer feel safe with the ones we love. And we no longer feel loved and free—at least not with our husbands.

Pardon my corny analogies, but some of us become turtles, hiding behind a shell to protect us from being hurt again. Some of us become volcanoes, spewing out hot lava of anger to anyone who dares not to meet our expectations. Some of us become flowers in a delicate vase, hoping our men will notice us, protect us, and handle us carefully. And some of us become like Superwoman, trying to right every wrong and solve every problem to show that we're really significant after all.

When this happens—when we fail to communicate—we stop feeling safe. And before long we're living emotionally separated from the men we vowed to share life with forever. Even worse, we might start pursuing those feelings of safety somewhere else. Our minds become consumed with a nightmare of "what ifs" and suspicions about what our husbands are thinking and doing. Or we move to a fantasy world and escape through daytime TV and romance novels. Or we find ourselves emotionally (maybe even physically) wrapped in someone else's arms. But nightmares, fantasies, and illicit dalliances are never satisfying substitutes for healthy relationships.

Where Do You Fit?

Consider these three roadblocks to effective communication, and ask yourself if any of them are hindering your progress in your most important human relationship—the one with the man you love:

1. Being so overloaded with responsibilities and commitments that you've lost sight of the simple things in life. Examine your commitments and determine what your priorities are and should be.

2. Being weighed down by shame, anger, or bitterness. Remember, we're as sick as our secrets. Identify them, pray about them, talk to a trusting girlfriend or mentor, and begin taking the steps to release the burden.

3. Not making time. Maybe you have time to talk with him, but you fill your time with phone calls, television, shopping trips, sports, friends, and other activities. When you shut your partner out like this, you compromise feelings of safety, and your love withers.

Feeling Safe

Let me trace this back for you. Genesis 2:25 says, "The man and his wife were both naked, and they felt no shame." Today we might say they were there for each other. This can happen for you only when you're feeling safe, and feeling safe includes having the courage to move toward your man in honesty and hope. Not just honesty—plenty of couples blast each other with "truth" about the other person's mistakes and annoying habits. That brand of honesty doesn't create understanding or stimulate love or safety—just broken hearts and resentment.

My Hope for You

In this book, we'll look at ten important issues in relationships. They explain why couples just don't talk—especially when life doesn't seem to be going the way it should. We'll examine topics that range from the past to the future, from the mundane to the sublime. If we learn to talk with our husbands more effectively, we'll feel more connected, more secure, and more loved. We won't let secrets poison our relationships because we'll deal with difficulties before they can cause real damage.

In these pages, you'll find some practical suggestions that will help you take the bold steps to begin important conversations, and you'll also discover some insights into the way men think (or don't think).

Five Ground Rules As We Get Started

1. You can't change him! The only person you can change is you. Your hope for a better tomorrow in Christ stares at you in the mirror every morning. When interacting with your husband, you can control only your own expectations, thoughts, words, and behaviors. You can speak the truth in love, offer to take a step deeper into intimacy, and see what happens. This is a journey you take one step at a time.

2. Change requires both of you. Even during conflict, discussions with your partner should be honest, respectful, and spoken in love (Ephesians 4:26,29,32). Try to keep your talk purposeful, goal-oriented, and free of hidden agendas. And be sensitive to timing (don't bring up a difficult situation at the dinner table). In volatile situations, this can be difficult. James 1:19 tells us to "be quick to listen, slow to speak and slow to become angry." Proverbs 18:13 points out the folly and shame of answering a matter before it's fully heard and understood.

I believe in spiritual intimacy because true growth as a couple is impossible apart from God. Reading a devotional together and praying together and for each other draw you closer to God and to each other.

3. Demands are not helpful. Some of us are deeply wounded, and hurt people often want others to step in and fix their hurts immediately and completely. Even just thinking about these issues can tempt some of us to start making demands. That, I assure you, won't improve your relationship with your husband. If you feel like making demands of him, step back, find a friend or counselor to talk with, and resolve some of the hurts that fuel those demands.

4. Loving someone requires humility, which is an attitude of the heart. The famous love passage, 1 Corinthians 13, describes love as patient and kind. It is not envious, proud, rude, self-seeking, or easily angered. It keeps no record of wrongs. It always protects, trusts, hopes, perseveres, and rejoices with truth. This passage exemplifies the attitude of the heart necessary for the marital relationship to be healthy and satisfying.

5. Let God do His work in your heart and life. He didn't make a mistake when He made us male and female, and He created marriage so two people could become one flesh. I believe God delights in every courageous step we take to be honest with Him and with our husbands about the things that are on our hearts, and He is thrilled when we are patient, kind, and forgiving along the way. Marriage is a complex matrix of desires, hopes, and choices. In some relationships, a minor adjustment can make a big difference, but others require a major overhaul. Be sure of this: God has you right where He wants you. He is good, strong, and kind, and He'll help you take steps to build a more loving and lasting connection with the man you love.

My goal for this book and my hope for you is that God will use the stories and insights to inspire you, challenge you, and encourage you. As you take even the smallest steps, you'll be building a foundation of trust. With that foundation, everything is possible; without it, nothing meaningful and good can happen. Understanding and trust create a wonderfully safe place where two people can explore each other, God's purposes, and the adventure of life more fully than ever. This kind of relationship stimulates creativity, salves daily hurts, and promotes laughter and love that carry us through the ups and downs of life.

Communication, safety, and love. That's what this book is about. I pray that God will give you insight and courage to walk this path with me.

I'm not telling him about...

1 My Frustrations About Him

The majority of husbands remind me of an orangutan trying to play the violin.

HONORÉ DE BALZAC

YOU'VE PLAYED THE GAME. Most girls I know have. Sometimes we play it as early as kindergarten. "He loves me, he loves me not...he loves me, he loves me not..." As daisy petals fall to the ground, a girl's heart falls in love. And usually it's not even about the boy. Even if he's not interested, she falls in love with the idea of being loved.

Fast-forward about 20 years. Kindergarten fantasies have gradually led to high hopes, great expectations, and the chapel of love. A bride walks down the aisle trusting that she has fallen in love with the man of her dreams. As she makes her approach, he's standing tall at the altar. Her dream has come true.

The wedding is spectacular (in most cases anyway). And the honeymoon...[censored]. Yes, the honeymoon is also amazing, but during that time a few suspicions begin to creep in, and she starts the "self talk": *No, he's not really like that.* Gradually, some of her fleeting suspicions prove true. A month or two after the wedding, she wakes up one morning, looks at the big hairy hulk next to her, and thinks, *What in the world have I done?*

When we realized life wouldn't be a fairy tale after all, some of us were devastated. But most of us simply lowered our expectations, closed our mouths (well, most of the time), and tried to make the best of things. Still, some of the frustration remains. We repress it as long and as hard as we can, but from time to time, those little annoying things our husbands do are like matches thrown into a barrel of gasoline—it isn't pretty!

> The honeymoon is the only period when a woman isn't trying to reform her husband.
>
> EVAN ESAR

Have you ever noticed that all of the serious problems in a woman's life start with the word *men? Men*struation, *men*opause, *men*tal illness…Well, maybe we can't blame those things on men, but here are a few comments women often make about men. They fall into two distinct categories: minor annoyances and genuine frustrations.

Minor Annoyances

When we were dating, most of us had no idea our future husbands would…

- use the last of the toilet paper and not replace it
- leave crumbs and pieces of chips on the sofa every night
- drink milk straight out of the jug and put it back in the refrigerator
- leave their dirty underwear all over the bedroom and bathroom

- make their towels smell like a toxic waste dump
- let their toothpaste squirt out on the counter and leave it there
- take three minutes to gulp down dinners we've spent hours to prepare
- say, "Huh?" when we've finished pouring out our hearts
- think we don't hear them (or smell them) pass a little gas whenever the urge arises
- believe that all these things are cute
- _____ (fill in the blank)

If you're like me, this "cute" behavior drives you up a wall. But through the years, I have learned that I have to be careful when I respond to minor annoyances. And remember, these are minor annoyances. Very few hills are worth dying on, and I can assure you, none of the things I've mentioned above make that short list. If you're hung up here, hold on because the water gets a lot deeper.

What's a Woman to Do?

Ladies, we have three options.

Option one. We can try to ignore what our husbands are doing and hope that somehow, with time, they will magically change. I've known lots of girls who thought that sloppy men who lived in close proximity with them would somehow change through the process of osmosis. Unfortunately, that's not going to happen. I know. I tried it, and it doesn't work. Tim needed more than osmosis or a fairy's wand. Silence and magic are poor problem-solving tools, but countless women try them every day.

> "My husband says he'll leave me if I don't stop shopping. Lord knows I'll miss him."

Option two. Most of us use this one—we nag. We think that if we tell them enough times, roll our eyes enough, and sigh enough, they will change. When saying it nicely doesn't work, we ratchet up the noise with a demanding tone of voice or pitiful pleading. Quite often, guys can't stand it. They give in and do what we ask them to do—for a day or a week or maybe even a month, but not for long. Not surprisingly, they resent us nagging them, and they become passive-aggressive or totally resistant. Our threats, demands, pleas, and other forms of nagging may have short-term benefits, but they always come at a steep long-term cost. Several times in the book of Proverbs, Solomon shares advice like this to men: "Better to live on a corner of the roof than share a house with a quarrelsome wife" (Proverbs 21:9).

Don't be misled. When a man feels obliged to acquiesce to the demands of a nagging wife, the relationship is usually damaged, not strengthened. Trust slowly erodes, and distance builds. He may stay in the house, but as Solomon said, life may be better for him on the roof! When we insist on nagging our men into submission, we compound minor issues with major relational problems of distance, avoidance, and eroded trust. Don't be the nagging wife with the husband on the roof. Your neighbors will start to wonder.

Option three. Speak the truth in love. A better way to handle a relatively minor annoyance is to determine how important the issue is to you and whether it's worth pursuing. If it is, go to your husband about it *in love,* explain your perspective, ask for change, and take what you get. Remember, this pertains to minor issues, not major ones. At some point, we have to accept people for who they are without demanding that they fit into the molds we create for them.

Yes, I know that lots of books out there talk about training men the way we'd train a dog. That may be clever, but it's destructive. My advice is to begin by making your list of things he does that annoy you. Then talk to him about the first one on the list—not the top hundred, not the top ten, and not even the top two—just one. Remember, you're not his mother; you're his wife. He needs to feel safe with you.

When you talk to him, take any tension out by saying something like this: "I know this is not a big deal to you, and it's not a big deal to me either, but I'd appreciate it if you'd…" If he's defensive, his response reveals an underlying tension in the relationship that's much more important than the annoying habit, and this tension needs to be addressed. Don't be alarmed. This is a wonderful moment to shift gears and talk about the two of you, your trust and communication, and what you both want in the relationship.

Too many women let small disappointments escalate into demands that cause serious harm in the relationship. Keep minor things minor. Talk about them, but never ever nag your man, especially in public. He'll feel disrespected. You'll feel rejected. And neither of you will benefit from it. Even if you get what you want, you lose.

Genuine Frustrations

For some of us, toothpaste, toilet paper, and underwear aren't even on the radar. Our sense of heartache goes much deeper. We're frustrated and hurt, and sometimes we feel like giving up. Women around the country have told me stories of deep disappointments. Here are a few.

> Love is like a puzzle. When you're in love, all the pieces fit; but when your heart gets broken, it takes a while to put everything back together.

1. "He's disengaged from me" or *"He's preoccupied with work."* Financial stress, wayward children, health problems, and a host of other difficulties can be the culprit, as well as being preoccupied with promotions and social climbing. He spends less time with you, and even when he's physically present, his mind seems a million miles away.

2. "He doesn't (or can't) communicate about the things that really matter to me." This may be the most common complaint among women. We long for our husbands to enter our worlds and talk about the things that mean the most to us. When we were dating, maybe they showed signs of being able to talk at a deep level, or maybe we assumed they would learn. Or maybe we just didn't realize how important this issue is. But now we feel hurt by their inability to connect with our hearts. And in our pain, we become more demanding, or we back away into our own world of friends who really understand us. Either way, we make the problem worse.

3.*"He takes me for granted."* Some women feel more like a combination of a maid and a prostitute than a cherished wife. No wonder we feel frustrated! A few words of appreciation mean the world to us, but when we don't hear them often enough, resentment creeps into our hearts. We can live with our husbands under the same roof and still feel emotionally abandoned. Psychologists tell us that abandonment can be as hard or harder to heal than abuse. When we're abandoned, we somehow assume we were never worthy of being loved in the first place.

4.*"He's domineering and demanding."* This is the opposite of the passive men who take no initiative with us. In this case, the men in our lives expect to be in the center of our worlds, waited on hand and foot. They may work hard and may even do a lot around the house, but they always expect their needs to be our first priority. We often admired this kind of man's strength when we were dating, but now it appears to be strength without love. Some women in this kind of relationship try to lower the level of conflict by becoming passive and compliant. Others become defiant and resistant—which creates an explosive mix that usually leads to damaged reputations and broken hearts.

5.*"When I pursue, he withdraws."* What is it about some men that they have to feel like they're in complete control? Why are certain conversations strictly off limits? They can be happy and confident until we say something innocent, like "Honey, I'd like to talk about something." Suddenly, at any notion of intimacy, they become weak and defensive and turn to their work, TV, buddies, the outdoors, or sports to feel safe.

Is There Hope?

Certainly these are major frustrations, but they don't have to ruin the relationship. The healing path for women relating to men like these includes grief, forgiveness, a new perspective, and better communication skills. Living with men who take us for granted, who are preoccupied with work or are depressed, who insist on being the center of the universe, or who can't communicate about important things hurts us deeply.

> God, grant me the serenity to accept the things I cannot change, the courage to change the things I can, and the wisdom to know the difference.
>
> SERENITY PRAYER

We sometimes think grief relates only to the death of someone we love, but we need to grieve all significant losses, including the wounds we've mentioned in this section of the chapter. As we are honest about the hurt we've experienced, we can choose to forgive the ones who hurt us. Forgiveness isn't a feeling; it's a choice to refuse to take revenge by gossiping about someone, verbally attacking him, or using any other weapon against him. Grief and forgiveness go hand in hand. Both involve honesty and courage, and both require a process of healing. If we stay with them, feelings of relief come sooner or later.

As we heal emotionally, we gain a new perspective. We learn to see the glass as half full instead of half empty. Resentment gradually gives way to thankfulness, and we learn to trust God to use every circumstance in our lives to shape us into the image of His Son. This is not an easy path, but God never promised that life would be easy—only that He would be with us and that He would use every experience for good in our lives, even those that are most painful and frustrating. In his book *The Healing Path,* psychologist Dan Allender describes the spiritual perception we can have about even the most painful events in our lives.

> If we fail to anticipate thoughtfully how we will respond to the harm of living in a fallen world, the pain may be for naught. It will either numb or destroy us rather than refine and even bless us…Healing in this life is not the resolution of our past; it is the use of our past to draw us into deeper relationship with God and His purposes for our lives.[1]

Few of us can gain this new, faith-filled perspective on our own. We need friends who have walked this road before us, or we need gifted counselors who can help us process the pain and find real hope for the future. God never intended for us to walk this difficult journey on our own. He gives us wonderful people who can help us take courageous steps.

> I haven't spoken to my wife in years. I didn't want to interrupt her.
> RODNEY DANGERFIELD

What You Can Say to Him

No, I haven't forgotten about this. The last piece of the puzzle is to gain important skills in communication. I recommend a simple but profound template: *I feel, I want, I will.*

When we want to communicate with men who frustrate us deeply, we can say something like this:

> I feel hurt [or angry or afraid or confused or whatever you really feel] when this happens [describe it clearly]. I want a relationship based on trust and respect, and I'm sure you

do too. I want to make a commitment to you today that I will value our relationship enough to be honest with you when I feel hurt so that we can resolve things between us before they escalate. I promise that I won't nitpick you to death. I just want to love you the best I can, and I want to be loved by you. I'll focus on really important things and change what I need to so we can both feel safe. Are you willing to join me?

And then listen. Your man will probably feel just as awkward about the conversation as you do, so don't expect perfection. Woody Allen says 90 percent of life is just showing up. Similarly, 90 percent of the success in these conversations is being in them. Don't worry if you don't say things perfectly or respond just right. And don't get upset if the first conversation doesn't completely solve all the trouble that's been brewing between you for many years! Take a step, speak the truth in love, and listen patiently.

And by the way, none of this will ever change if you're not first willing to give up blame—of yourself and him. Some of us become blame sponges, soaking up all the responsibility in order to lower the level of conflict and get it over with as quickly as possible. Others of us are blame throwers, accusing others and refusing to accept any share of the responsibility. Be honest with yourself about this. Which kind of person are you? Who are you more likely to cast blame on, and when are you most likely to do it? Take a moment to consider what adjustments you might need to make.

Remember, you won't change him. First focus on yourself and do not demand change from him. Assign appropriate responsibility, accept your part of the problem, and apologize for your sins and errors. This process has no guarantee, but quite often when one person says, "I'm sorry," the other person feels free to lower his or her defenses and accept responsibility too.

The "pounce factor" is a destructive dynamic in difficult relationships.

When one person becomes vulnerable or indecisive—sometimes even for just a second—an intimidating person may take the opportunity to pounce. We see this happen in all kinds of relationships: with other women, at work, and at home. Victims may give in or get away to stop the attack, but they will remember— oh yes, they will remember.

> I praise loudly,
> I blame softly.
> CATHERINE THE GREAT

And this dynamic is not limited to power-hungry men who pounce on weak wives. Men may be lions at work, but when they walk in the door and realize they've entered the presence of a lion tamer, they may become passive or resistant. Either response can cause them to boil with anger. Pouncing doesn't always include bared fangs and glaring eyes. Some women pounce on their men with their incessant whining, pitiful demands, and unrealistic expectations of attention and affection.

Pain raises the level of demands, and this is one of the major problems in strained relationships. The more we hurt, the more we expect the people who hurt us to fix our pain. When they fail (or we perceive them as failing), we feel even more hurt, and our demands escalate accordingly. As you can tell, that simply doesn't make sense, but many of us follow this path as if it were the gospel. Instead of looking to men to fill our hearts, we need to look first to the Lord, the one who knows us intimately, who loves us deeply, and who is present with us at all times. Our deepest need is to know Him, and He is our greatest source of wisdom and strength as we relate to the men in our lives.

The Ideal Spouse

Think about this question for a moment: What is the greatest thing you lose when you get married? For most women, things like independence, autonomy, financial freedom, and time with friends and family come to mind. And to some degree we do lose these things.

Our decisions no longer affect us alone; they affect our husbands too. Compromise becomes part of our everyday lives.

But whether our disappointments are minor or major, our frustrations relatively mild or devastating, we women inevitably lose something else when we commit to our men. We may recognize it in premarital counseling, but too often, we're still starry-eyed at that point. Most of us don't sense this loss until a month or two after we get back from the honeymoon. We wake up, look at our man, and wonder what we've done. At that moment, we sense deep in our souls that a dream is shattered. We've lost our sense of the ideal husband.

So how are things going with your Prince Charming? My guess is that you have had plenty of disappointments along the way. I hope they've all been minor annoyances, but perhaps they're deeper and more troubling than that. When you bump into small ones, don't nag your husband into submission. I tried that with Tim in the first few years of our marriage and realized after a brief separation and far too many tears that nagging was never going to work. Accept your man the way he is, but with a spirit of love, feel free to ask him for a change in one area that bothers you. If you see a new, positive habit form, talk about another one after a significant amount of time has passed. (Give him more than just a day or a week!)

Does Christ Roll His Eyes at You?

Paul wrote to the Romans, "Accept one another, then, just as Christ accepted you, in order to bring praise to God" (Romans 15:7). How does Christ accept you? Does He roll His eyes when you do something He doesn't appreciate? In the Gospel accounts, did He nag people so much that they finally agreed to do what He wanted them to do? Not hardly. He saw through many sins and mistakes, and He focused on their hearts. That's what matters to Him about you, and as you and I experience more of His love, acceptance, and forgiveness, the hearts of the men in our lives will matter much more than their insignificant idiosyncrasies.

But if the men in our lives are causing much deeper hurts, we need to go deeper into the love and wisdom of God to know how to respond. We still need to love and accept them, but loving them includes speaking the truth in love and offering a path toward genuine understanding and feelings of safety. The road may be long and hard, but if people are willing to stay on it, miracles can happen. I know. I've seen it in my relationship with Tim.

In the Word: Chapter One Application

Drive-through burgers, fast-cash ATMs, handy little instant coffee packets...without a doubt, we live in a fast-paced culture. We want what we want when we want it—and when is *now!* Instantly! And that includes the change we expect to see in our men's lives. We talk ourselves into believing they will change. *Maybe if I just sleep backward tonight in my bed with my feet at the headboard, I'll wake up tomorrow and he'll have changed!* Sounds crazy, I know, but so does our belief that we can change them. When our expectations aren't met and they keep doing the same things over and over again, we get frustrated.

If you hold on to the belief that *he* is responsible to make you happy, you'll never be in a good mood when you wake up in the morning—at least not when you roll over to a grumpy husband, PMS, or a sick child. But think about this: How realistic are we being when we wait for our husbands to make the first move or when we expect the annoyances and frustrations we've talked about to merely disappear?

A good marriage takes time, wisdom, prayer, and commitment. And here's the great news: It *can* happen! I know it can, because God's Word says so. God created marriage to be a beautiful, wonderful, and fulfilling relationship, but it also has the potential to be hellish. What's the difference? It starts by looking inward. As we discussed in this chapter, annoyances and frustrations can create a lot of conflict.

In this next section, let's get in the Word of God and find practical ways to handle our frustrations.

Who You Are

Your name may be Mrs. Smith, Mrs. Brown, or Mrs. MacGhilleseatheanaich (a real name!), but you can know that you are far more than just Mrs. So-and-So. If you are a believer in Jesus Christ, God's Word says that you are a daughter of God: "How great is the love the Father has lavished on us, that we should be called children of God!" (1 John 3:1). Take a moment and say these truths aloud—three times: "God says I am precious and honored in His sight, and He has loved me with an everlasting love." (See Isaiah 43:4 and Jeremiah 31:1.) You are royalty! In fact, God's Word is full of statements about who you are as His child. Here are a few more you can speak out loud.

- "I am God's workmanship" (Ephesians 2:10).
- "I am a co-heir with Christ" (Romans 8:17).
- "I am more than a conqueror through Christ" (Romans 8:37).
- "I am completely forgiven" (Ephesians 1:7).
- "I am free from the law of sin and death" (Romans 8:2).
- "I am the righteousness of God in Christ Jesus" (2 Corinthians 5:21).

We can easily fall into the trap of defining ourselves by our relationship with our men, but when we truly grasp that *this* is who we are, we begin to see our men differently too. If we place our identity in the men we love, we will continually feel the compulsive need to be affirmed by them. That puts us in a precarious position because we depend on them for our happiness. Our frustrations can easily get blown out of proportion when our men's simple mistakes shatter our fragile worlds!

The Power of Your Words

The average human tongue weighs 60 to 70 grams, but the funny thing is, very few of us are able to hold our tongues! "The tongue has the power of life and death" (Proverbs 18:21). Okay, so maybe you haven't *killed* anyone with your tongue, but God's Word emphasizes repeatedly just how powerful our words are—for good or for evil.

> The tongue is a small part of the body, but it makes great boasts. Consider what a great forest is set on fire by a small spark. The tongue also is a fire, a world of evil among the parts of the body. It corrupts the whole person, sets the whole course of his life on fire, and is itself set on fire by hell. All kinds of animals, birds, reptiles and creatures of the sea are being tamed and have been tamed by man, but no man can tame the tongue. It is a restless evil, full of deadly poison (James 3:5-8).

That's why Paul tells the believers in the Ephesian church to check their own tongues and not to point the finger: "Do not let any unwholesome talk come out of your mouths, but only what is helpful for building others up according to their needs, that it may benefit those who listen" (Ephesians 4:29).

Think about the power you have either to beat up your husband or to build him up. His attitude and feelings of safety in the relationship often rise and fall on whether he feels like a failure or like someone who could take on the world. Trust me; you want a man who can take on the world.

In the battle for our relationships, our most powerful weapons may be our tongues. When our words are hateful or hurtful, we "grieve the Holy Spirit of God" (Ephesians 4:30). Rather than nagging and continually pointing out our men's quirks, we need to consciously choose to encourage them more than we criticize them. Here are a few ways we can do that:

- Be a good listener (James 1:19).

- Reflect and think through what he says (Proverbs 15:23).

- Be sensitive and respectful (Ephesians 4:31). Respect is his relational fuel!

- Speak the truth—but always in love. Tone down the emotions (Colossians 3:9).

- Don't respond in anger (Ephesians 4:26,31).

- Confess and forgive (Ephesians 4:32).

You might be thinking, *Julie, you just don't know him. He is so annoying sometimes!* I understand—as I said, holding our tongues is not easy. Tim can be *so* high maintenance at times. (Sorry, honey.) A lot of times, stopping myself from saying those cutting remarks is the last thing I want to do. But Paul says that it all goes back to God. God forgave us (Ephesians 4:32), so we can follow His example by setting aside our desire to prove our husbands wrong and by extending love to them through what we *don't* say and what we *do* say.

The F-Word: *Fight*

Fighting is the one of the things we wives are most afraid of. But allow me to let you in on something: Every marriage has frustrations. Every marriage has conflict. The question is not *do* you disagree and fight, but *how* do you fight? Being caring and considerate is easy in the romantic moments, but under pressure, difficult emotions can fly wild. They can be as messy as a pot that boils over or a tube of toothpaste that gets squeezed too hard. In these moments, when the last thing we want to do is to love our husbands, we need to stop and take a deep breath!

Rather than blowing up, accusing them, or shutting down, we must make the conscious choice to set aside our emotions for a second and get the big picture. The apostle Paul writes, "Do nothing out of selfish ambition or vain conceit, but in humility consider others better than yourselves. Each of you should look not only to your own interests, but also to the interests of others" (Philippians 2:3-4).

Paul isn't saying we should devalue ourselves. Rather, he's saying we all need a healthy dose of otherness in our lives. Face it—naturally, we tend to think about ourselves a lot. A whole lot. You may be thinking, *Nice. But I don't* want *to think about that jerk first. I have to look out for myself.*

Realize that your relationship is bigger than just the two of you. Paul goes on to write, "Your attitude should be the same as that of Christ Jesus: Who, being in very nature God, did not consider equality with God something to be grasped, but made himself nothing, taking the very nature of a servant" (verses 5-7). Jesus spent His entire earthly life serving other people even though He was the God of the universe!

Fights scare us, but did you know that God encourages us wives to fight? That's right. God wants us to fight for our marriages by maintaining healthy attitudes every day. Hell is against every relationship that has the potential to bring glory to God. It's a fight, ladies, but there's nothing better to spend your life fighting for than a marriage that brings glory to Jesus.

So then, what does the right kind of fighting look like? We have to make the choice every single day to value our husbands in spite of the burps, crumbs, and dirty underwear. Our culture depicts love as a feeling of passion, and we've all enjoyed that sensation as we've looked deep into our husbands' eyes. But all of us know that on some days, the sparks just aren't there! Compared with God's description of love, the world's imitation is pretty cheap.

Getting My Needs Met

Don't you just wish sometimes that you had a credit card with no limit and no interest? I do. Especially on those days when every single thing that could go wrong seems to go wrong! When I am down, I can easily start expecting Tim to make everything better—to meet all of my needs.

Let's see what God's Word says: "My God will meet all your needs according to his glorious riches in Christ Jesus" (Philippians 4:19). Who is the only one who has guaranteed to meet our needs? God! As much as we love our guys, they are not perfect. (Surprise!) And they never will be. When we realize that only God can meet our deepest longings, we are free from our need to place unrealistic expectations on our husbands. Remember, they are not supermen! They are sinful human beings just like us, and they will make mistakes, mess up, and hurt us sometimes.

The good news is that what God starts, He always finishes. Just like you, your husband is a work in progress. He's a construction zone. God's Word says that "he who began a good work in you will carry it on to completion until the day of Christ Jesus" (Philippians 1:6).

Every time I find toothpaste in the sink or the toilet seat up, I have to remind myself that I am not the one who is responsible for changing Tim. My job is to honestly express what I'm feeling in a loving way. And then I can rest in knowing that God is at work.

Reflection Questions

1. What (or who) defines who you are? Your husband? Your kids? Your job? Are you looking to your husband to "make everything better" in your life rather than looking to God for encouragement, help, and direction? Are you worshipping at the altar of the ideal spouse?

2. What are your husband's most annoying habits? Take some time to write out the little things that aggravate you. On a separate list, write out the "biggies"—the genuine frustrations that drive you up the wall.

3. In this chapter, we talked about three ways we commonly respond to being frustrated—we ignore, we nag, or we speak the truth in love. How have you been responding to the frustrations you have with your husband? Are you using your words to build your husband up or tear him down?

4. Pick one of your husband's most annoying habits. Have you talked to him about it? How can you begin today to lovingly address this conflict?

I'm not telling him about. . .

2 My Fears About Money and Security

*No matter how hard you hug your money,
it never hugs back.*

QUOTED IN P.S. I LOVE YOU,
COMPILED BY H. JACKSON BROWN, JR.

WHAT IS THE NUMBER ONE REASON for marital tension and divorce? Is it bad sex, poor communication, differing parenting styles, infidelity, or pornography? No, experts agree that none of these create the most problems for couples. Money does.

We women often have a very different view of money than men do, and this can cause problems. When we date, those differences seem cute, or at least they're not a big concern. But as soon as we get back from the honeymoon and start paying bills, these differences can become wedges between us. And financial worries aren't isolated to the single issue of the checkbook. They are part of a complex web of perceptions, values, and goals that permeate every other area of our lives: the way we raise children, how we relate to in-laws, the way we communicate, and what happens between the sheets. Yes, even what happens in the bedroom. A British study led by psychologist Thomas Pollet of Newcastle University reports that the frequency of women's orgasms increases as financial strains with her partner subside through increases in income.[1] Finding peace in the area of finances brings joy in every area of life.

> The safe way to double your money is to fold it over once and put it in your pocket.
>
> FRANK HUBBARD

Different, Really Different

Maybe our perspectives about money are wired into our DNA, or maybe men have absorbed them from their dads and women from our moms, but men and women view money quite distinctly. Here's what a study by Jay McDonald revealed:

> Women, trained to nurture and seek acceptance, view money as a means to create a lifestyle. Women spend on things that enhance day-to-day living. Theirs is a now-money orientation.
>
> Men, trained to fix and provide, view money as a means to capture and accumulate value. Men don't spend, they invest. Men don't want something, they need it. Theirs is a future-money orientation.[2]

In the same article, McDonald quotes Ruth Hayden, financial counselor and author of *For Richer, Not Poorer: The Money Book for Couples*. Hayden observed that women instinctively spend money on their children and their lifestyle, but men focus their financial interests in investments such as homes or retirement accounts.

Women are the collectors of stuff. Women do the clothes.
Women are taught that what they need to get through life
is approval. They have to look good, act good, be good...
When men go shopping, they expect that whatever they're
shopping for to 'get fixed,' because men are supposed to fix
stuff. They don't want to be part of the process.

This isn't just a bland observation by a person doing research in
an ivory tower. Financial counselors see these differences played out
in meetings with couples all day every day. Husbands and wives have
different priorities, different perspectives, and different choices about
what to do with their money. If they don't understand these differences and communicate often and clearly, they're almost certainly
headed for turmoil.

One of the principles marriage counselors observe is that the more
money a couple has, the less tension they experience, so they fight less
over money. They may fight like cats and dogs over their children, sex,
or in-laws, but they tend to argue less about finances if they have ample
money in the bank. Couples that are deeply in debt or barely getting
by, however, experience frequent and heated exchanges.

One of the biggest problems is that the couple may not agree on how
much money they have and how much they are spending. A study of
married men and women for the *Journal of Socio-Economics* by Ohio
State University researcher Jay Zagorsky found that one-third of couples agreed on their level of debt, income, and net worth, one-third
disagreed to a small degree, but one-third had wildly different views.
To the extent that they believe different things about their finances,
their expectations and disagreements escalate.

Expectations of Plenty

Couples have always been susceptible to differences in perceptions and
expectations, but today's young couples find it very easy to miss each other.

For them, expectations and reality can clash violently. Many 20-somethings have grown up enjoying the benefits of a full lifestyle. Even homes with modest incomes included a cell phone, an Xbox or Game Boy, an MP3 player, a PDA, the latest computer, and of course, trendy clothes and all kinds of entertainment. They went to college expecting an ever-upward climb of wealth and enjoyment, but graduation and work has disappointed many of them.

> **Wealth:** any income that is at least one hundred dollars more a year than the income of one's wife's sister's husband.
>
> H.L. MENCKEN

Psychologist Jean Twenge, a professor at San Diego State University, wrote a book called *Generation Me: Why Today's Young Americans Are More Confident, Assertive, Entitled—and More Miserable Than Ever Before.* She notes, "There are a lot of young people hitting 25 who are making, say $35,000 a year, who expected they'd be millionaires or at least making six figures."[3] Many of these young adults spend every penny they make, and they live on the financial edge every month. When they face unanticipated expenses, like car repairs or roommates leaving them with the full apartment payment, they have to go into debt to pay for them.

Those of us who are a little older shouldn't shake our heads at the younger generation. Some of us have done a great job saving and investing for retirement, but many of us live just as much on the edge as our kids who just graduated from college. We want to look as if we're as successful as the next couple, so we buy new cars, fine homes, and the latest gadgets to prove we're keeping up. Many of us have virtually no savings, certainly not several months of salary saved for emergency expenses and a growing retirement account. No, just like the younger generation, many of us focus on today, not tomorrow.

For example, some of the people who aren't putting a dime into a 401(k) or any other type of retirement account nonetheless somehow believe that their ship will come in someday. The annual Retirement Confidence Survey reports that almost half of the people who haven't saved any money for retirement are "somewhat confident" they will live comfortably after they retire. Maybe they're counting on a big inheritance, or maybe they believe something magical will happen to give them the income they'll need.[4]

Four Kinds of Couples

In his insightful book *Make Your Money Count,* financial planner Jim Munchbach identifies four distinctly different scenarios of how couples manage—or mismanage—their money.[5] Each situation requires unique financial goals and decisions.

Buried in Debt

We may think of people on welfare as those who are chronically in debt, but that's not the only group that's under water financially. In fact, some couples with enormous incomes chronically spend much more than they make. Even doctors, attorneys, and wildly successful businesspeople can find themselves buried in debt. Most of them became enamored with an extravagant lifestyle, and their goal was to keep up with the Gateses instead of the Joneses.

Other high-income families got into debt through circumstances beyond their control. A friend of mine and her husband lived well within their income for many years, but their daughter experienced a life-threatening disease that consumed two years of their lives and all of their savings. The medical bills far surpassed their insurance, and they looked at a final bill of more than half a million dollars. They eventually settled with the doctors and the hospital for much less, but they still had to spend years paying off the debt.

Many people who are in deep debt believe that somebody somewhere is going to come through for them and bail them out. They daydream about winning the lottery, or they imagine that a rich aunt will change her will and give all her money to them instead of their cousins.

Consumer debt has a nasty habit of escalating because credit card companies raise interest rates whenever someone misses a payment on any bill they owe. Before long, the debt becomes insurmountable, and the couple feels hopeless.

Whatever the cause, people who are buried in debt need to focus on getting their heads out of the financial mud so they can breathe a bit easier again. Drastic changes in thinking and acting are often required, and both the husband and wife need to agree on the solution for it to work.

Barely Above Water

Many couples carefully look at their income stream, and they craft their budget to spend absolutely every dime! By the end of the month, some of these couples determine which restaurant to go to and the size of the popcorn box to buy at the movie based on how much is left in their account. They roll along on the edge for a long time—until an unexpected expense ruins their world. It doesn't take much: a car repair, a roof leak, a medical bill, a traffic ticket, damage from a fire or a storm…almost anything can pop up and push them over the edge.

Many young couples try to balance financial responsibility with having fun and setting up their apartments or new homes. Because they're starting out, they have additional expenses. Too often, they buy new cars with large payments because they don't want to look dorky to their friends who have just bought the latest models.

When wise parents try to talk to these couples about financial planning and saving for retirement, they often respond, "We can't even think about that because we don't have any money." That's precisely the problem, not the answer.

Bucks in the Bank but Still Worried

Many couples have saved some money for unexpected expenses and retirement, but they worry that they don't have enough. In difficult economic times, when their mutual funds decline, they wake up at night in a cold sweat!

Others, though, have plenty of money, far more than they'll ever need, but they don't know what their lives are about. Without a sense of purpose, the only measure of success is accumulating more money, buying more possessions, and enjoying more extravagant vacations. Their worry isn't that they won't have enough, but that they'll come to the end of their lives and find the box is empty.

No amount of money, possessions, or pleasure can fill the hole in our hearts. Only Christ can do that, and He's more than willing if we'll let Him. When we experience His love, He gives us direction and purpose. Then our money comes into focus. We don't spend it only on our wants, but we invest a significant part of it for His kingdom. Couples who use their money together to honor God are the most fulfilled of any I know. They are in the fourth and final group.

Full of Purpose and Contentment

A few couples in every community really "get it." Their lives aren't about things; they thrive on relationships. They've devoted themselves to making a difference in people's lives, and they love seeing God use them. They may not have millions of dollars, but they see every dime that comes their way as a gift from God. Even their talent to earn money is God's gift to them, so they thank God for their salary, their investments, their inheritance, and every other source of income.

I know people in all four of these categories, and Tim and I have lived for a time in all of them too. The worry factor declines from one category to the next as wisdom and purpose shape the grid we use to make decisions. We won't find true fulfillment and security in money because we'll never think we have enough. But if we find true joy in Christ, He'll give us wisdom to earn, save, invest, and give our money in ways that double our joy. Still, we need to become partners with our husbands for this to happen.

Can't Always Blame Him

Blaming our husbands for spending more than our household incomes would be a convenient way to approach the problem, but we need to look closely in the mirror and be honest about what we see. I once heard that a man uses five things in the bathroom: a razor, shaving cream, toothpaste, toothbrush, and soap. Women average ten times as many items, and their men couldn't identify most of them!

> A man will pay $2 for a $1 item he wants. A woman will pay $1 for a $2 item she doesn't want!

As we've seen in other chapters, we live in a culture of comparisons. We're always checking ourselves out—not our character, but our hair, clothes, cars, children's achievements, and every other external thing around us. Having nice things isn't enough for us—our things must be nicer than someone else's! Who is this other person? For most of us, she's a phantom woman, a collage of the woman with the nicest figure, the finest clothes, the most stylish car, the most gorgeous hair, the most successful husband, the cutest shoes, and everything else we can possibly compare. These desires create incredibly high expectations and tremendous discontent unless we successfully measure up. But regardless of how many of these battles we win, we ultimately lose the war because somebody always has more than we have, and our desires and fears absorb our thoughts, consume our hearts, and harm our most cherished relationships. So, ladies, the first part of the remedy is to be honest about the role we play in the relationship by wanting (or demanding) too much.

The average person in America today owes about $10,000 in consumer debt, and for some, this figure is far higher. Many people struggle to pay the minimum each month, and they are saddled with incredibly high interest rates on their credit cards. A newspaper columnist who writes about personal finances received a letter from someone who admitted paying almost 30 percent interest on $12,000 in unsecured debt. The person tried to pay a little more than the minimum, "but the balance never goes down."

The columnist responded with the discouraging news that at the current rate of payments, the person would take more than 30 years to pay off his debt—and that's if he didn't buy anything else on credit in those 30 years.[6] When a husband, a wife, or both are lying awake at night trying to figure out how to make the next payment—or which payment to make this month and which to skip—debt consumes their thoughts and robs them of joy, love, and life.

Is Money a Spiritual Issue?

Jesus said more about the issue of money than any other topic—more than heaven, more than hell, and more than relationships. He wasn't preoccupied with money for money's sake. Rather, He knew that the way we handle money is a reflection of our deepest desires and our most closely held convictions. The numbers in our checkbook each month speak volumes about our

> Money can't buy happiness, but it can buy you the kind of misery you prefer.

priorities, our contentment, and our trust in God.

Author and speaker Elisabeth Elliot has incredible insights about spiritual life. She encourages us to loosen our grip on money so our hands can grasp something far more valuable. In *Keep a Quiet Heart,* she wrote this:

Money holds terrible power when it is loved. It can blind
us, shackle us, fill us with anxiety and fear, torment our
days and nights with misery, wear us out with chasing it...
Poverty has not been my experience, but God has allowed
in the lives of each of us some sort of loss, the withdrawal
of something we valued, in order that we may learn to offer
ourselves a little more willingly, to allow the touch of death
on one more thing we have clutched so tightly, and thus
know fullness and freedom and joy that much sooner.[7]

Having God's perspective on money is the first and most important step we can take toward financial freedom. Paul warned us, "For
the love of money is a root of all kinds of evil" (1 Timothy 6:10), and
King Solomon, who knew something about the empty promises of
wealth, wrote that "the sleep of a laborer is sweet, whether he eats
little or much; but the abundance of a rich man permits him no sleep"
(Ecclesiastes 5:12).

What Tithing Means

Over the years, most of us have heard dozens of sermons about
tithing, but some of these messages, I'm afraid, have missed God's
heart. Some well-meaning pastors have said that God wants us to
give 10 percent to Him and His church, but they sometimes leave the
impression that we can do whatever we want with the rest of it and
be as self-absorbed as we desire. That, I'm convinced, is a misunderstanding of the heart of the gospel. We don't owe God 10 percent of
ourselves. We owe Him everything we are and have.

The way we handle money is, according to Jesus, an outward expression of our inward convictions. Our primary focus, then, should be to
get our convictions right. The message of grace is that we were hope-
lessly lost and even enemies of God. But God, being rich in mercy,
loved us, forgave us, and adopted us as His beloved children. Paul tells

us that we've been bought with the price of Christ's death on the cross, so we're no longer our own. We belong to him.

In his challenging book *The Call,* author Os Guinness defines our purpose as "the truth that God calls us to himself so decisively that everything we are, everything we do, and everything we have is invested with a special devotion and dynamism lived out as a response to his summons and service."[8] Everything. Our time? Yes. Our relationships? Certainly. Every dime we earn, save, invest, or spend? Absolutely. God has given us the ability to earn a living. All we are and all we have is unreservedly and completely His. To use everything (even and especially our money) in a way that pleases Him is our privilege and pleasure.

When our perspective about God's grace permeates every fiber of our lives, we relax our demands for more because we're so thankful for what God has already given us. We aren't driven to go deeper into debt to prove ourselves to other people, so we have more money to save, invest, and spend on the things that really matter. And in response to God's marvelous gift to us, we'll give more and give gladly. Bestselling author and leadership expert Ken Blanchard and Chick-fil-A founder Truett Cathy identify the joy of giving in their book *The Generosity Factor:*

> There is a route to genuine and enduring satisfaction, but it flies in the face of this greedy, self-obsessed culture. It's called generosity, and it involves freely giving our four most valuable resources—our time, talents, treasure, and touch—and receiving unimaginable riches in return.[9]

Yes, it's true that men and women think and act very differently about money, but these differences are minimized when two people delight in the grace of God and pattern their lives by His wisdom and purposes. A focus on God empowers them to find common ground and follow the beliefs they share rather than fighting about their differences.

As you think about any tension that exists between you and your man over the issue of money, begin by focusing on your own heart. Examine your beliefs and your habits, and see how they measure up with the principles in this chapter. Enjoy the matchless grace of God, and trust Him to give you wisdom, joy, and generosity. Then you'll be ready to talk to your man about money and the particular kind of security it can provide.

What You Can Say to Him

Where has complaining and nagging about money gotten you in your relationship with your husband or boyfriend? You may have gotten a few things you wanted, but my guess is that you've lost some things that are far more precious: understanding, safety, and closeness. If you've been dissatisfied with the amount of money that he makes or that is available for you to spend, consider using the first conversation to talk about your own faults.

In an interview with Luci Shaw for *Radix* magazine, Dallas Willard, author of *The Divine Conspiracy,* reflected on the impact of uninhibited consumption in our culture:

> We are designed to be creators, initiators, not just receivers. Yet the whole model, the consumerist model of the human being, is to make us passive, and to make us complainers and whiners because we're not being given what we need. We cook up a "right" to that and then we say we've been deprived of our rights.[10]

If you've demanded your "right" to have more and more, take the first step to share your new insights and apologize for complaining. (Be sure to catch your man when he faints.) Invite him to examine your budget with you to see where the money is coming from and where it's going. Don't be defensive and don't be demanding. Blaming each other certainly won't help solve the financial problem, and it won't bring you closer together. Look at your budget honestly and objectively, and negotiate a workable, effective plan. Make a commitment to live within your means and pay off consumer debt. Many excellent resources are available to help individuals and couples communicate and develop a financial game plan, including Dave Ramsey and Crown Financial Services. Don't be afraid to get the help you need.

The biggest sources of conflict about money in a marriage occur when people don't talk, they make assumptions, and they get angry when other people don't act according to their unspoken assumptions. As the anger builds, they may explode in rage and blame, or they may withdraw into furious silence. Or they could alternate between these two. At any rate, don't let the backlog of painful emotions keep you from beginning this important conversation.

You may want to start by saying, "I know this has been a difficult subject for us, but I'd like to talk with you about our financial situation. First, I want to say I'm sorry for spending too much and demanding too much [or whatever your errors have been]. I want us to find a solution together so that money is something that brings us closer together and doesn't drive us apart." If he knows you aren't going to demand more and blame him, he'll probably be much more open to talk about money and the relational issues surrounding it.

The plan you work out will include several key ingredients, such as savings and investments, but those may not be priorities until you are out of debt. At all costs, don't borrow any more money until the current debt is paid, and even then, consider saving enough money to purchase things later rather than incurring more consumer debt now.

Make financial progress a glorious adventure. Some of us live with such resentment and anxiety over this issue that we can hardly imagine what a glorious adventure might look like, but I assure you, it's possible. When couples come together around a common goal and a workable financial plan, they support and encourage each other and stop complaining. When that happens, they work hard to dig themselves out of a hole, celebrate every victory, and offer help to each other when one is weak.

Some of us are gifted at setting good, clear goals, but others need some help. Popular author and speaker Brian Tracy highlights the importance of setting goals:

> Successful men and women invest the time necessary to develop absolute clarity about themselves and what they really want, like designing a detailed blueprint for a building before they begin construction. Most people just throw themselves at life like a dog chasing a passing car and wonder why they never seem to catch anything or keep anything worthwhile.[11]

Instead of despising the different ways you think about money, appreciate them. God made two people to become one, perfected in unity. This means that immediate financial goals as well as future financial goals are necessary for a healthy couple and a strong family.

Above all, let your communication about money turn into thankfulness. Give thanks to God for His goodness and faithfulness. Even when you're buried in debt, you can thank Him for the wisdom of the Scriptures and the hope He gives for progress out of the problem. Show your appreciation to your man for his hard work and his diligence to provide for the family, even if he doesn't make as much money as you'd like him to make. And give thanks to God and to your man every day as you take steps to get out of debt, build your savings, spend wisely, and invest for the future.

In the Word: Chapter Two Application

Dave Ramsey claims that money is mentioned more than 800 times in the Bible. Clearly, God cares a lot about the way we think about and use money. No one knows the heart of man better than God, which is why He focused so much on this topic. He knows about materialism's power to shape our hearts and destroy our lives. To have financial freedom and security, we must take God's advice to heart and manage our finances accordingly.

Is Money a Spiritual Issue?

Let's take a look at what the Bible says:

- "Do not wear yourself out to get rich; have the wisdom to show restraint. Cast but a glance at riches, and they are gone, for they will surely sprout wings and fly off to the sky like an eagle" (Proverbs 23:4-5).

- "Listen, my dear brothers: Has not God chosen those who are poor in the eyes of the world to be rich in faith and to inherit the kingdom he promised those who love him?" (James 2:5).

- "Command those who are rich in this present world not to be arrogant nor to put their hope in wealth, which is so uncertain, but to put their hope in God, who richly provides us with everything for our enjoyment. Command them to do good, to be rich in good deeds, and to be generous and willing to share. In this way they will lay up treasure for themselves as a firm foundation for the coming age, so that they may take hold of the life that is truly life" (1 Timothy 6:17-19).

- "Whoever trusts in his riches will fall, but the righteous will thrive like a green leaf" (Proverbs 11:28).

- "A faithful man will be richly blessed, but one eager to get rich will not go unpunished" (Proverbs 28:20).

- "Wealth is worthless in the day of wrath, but righteousness delivers from death" (Proverbs 11:4).

- "Whoever loves money never has money enough; whoever

loves wealth is never satisfied with his income" (Ecclesiastes 5:10).

• "A stingy man is eager to get rich and is unaware that poverty awaits him" (Proverbs 28:22).

• "Better a little with the fear of the LORD than great wealth
with turmoil" (Proverbs 15:16).

• "Better a poor man whose walk is blameless than a rich
man whose ways are perverse" (Proverbs 28:6).

The recurring theme in these passages is easy to see—money should
not be our main concern, and to be rich should not be our main goal in
life. The apostle Paul warns Timothy, "For the love of money is a root
of all kinds of evil. Some people, eager for money, have wandered from
the faith and pierced themselves with many griefs" (1 Timothy 6:10).

American society clearly revolves around the dollar. In order to eat,
you need to buy food. In order to drive your car, you need to buy gas.
You need money to live in a house and buy clothes and pay for utili-
ties…and the list goes on. When money becomes the foundation of
our very existence, our desires for riches can be very difficult to control.
We can be thankful that God did not remain silent on this issue.

Talk, Talk, Talk

Jay MacDonald made a wise observation when he said, "If couples
would do nothing more than sit down and discuss money with each
other, their chances of a long and happy life together would likely
increase dramatically."[12] This entire book is based on helping you learn
to discuss your deepest needs and desires with the man in your life. And
as we've seen, money is the number one reason for marital tension and
divorce, so we need effective communication about our finances!

Solomon writes, "A man finds joy in giving an apt reply—and
how good is a timely word!" (Proverbs 15:23). We are created to be
relational beings, and healthy communication is at the heart of strong

relationships. Men and women have unique approaches in many aspects of life, so we shouldn't be surprised to find various points of view about money and spending. Couples need to explore these differences together in conversation.

Many great books have been written on financial security, investing, spending, and debt reduction. You can find numerous websites for companies specializing in money management. I encourage you to learn all you can about how money impacts your life and functioning.

However, go to the Bible first and give it the highest priority. Find the verses that talk about money. Use a topical commentary if necessary. Know and understand God's way before seeking the world's view on economics and finances. Research together—as a couple!

Treasures of the Heart

> Do not store up for yourselves treasures on earth, where moth and rust destroy, and where thieves break in and steal. But store up for yourselves treasures in heaven, where moth and rust do not destroy, and where thieves do not break in and steal. For where your treasure is, there your heart will be also (Matthew 6:19-21).

Where is your treasure? When we leave this world behind, we will take nothing with us. Solomon writes, "Yet when I surveyed all that my hands had done and what I had toiled to achieve, everything was meaningless, a chasing after the wind; nothing was gained under the sun" (Ecclesiastes 2:11).

Where is your heart? "No servant can serve two masters. Either he will hate the one and love the other, or he will be devoted to the one and despise the other. You cannot serve both God and Money" (Luke 6:13). I love Hebrews 13:5: "Keep your lives free from love of money and be content with what you have, because God has said, 'Never will I leave you; never will I forsake you.'"

Learn to rest in God's provision and protection regardless of your financial circumstances. Whether you are in times of plenty or times of need, He will be there and will provide for you. Do not give in to the way of the world and its love of money. Give God your fears and relinquish control into His capable hands. Trust and believe this truth found in Philippians 4:19: "And my God will meet all your needs according to his glorious riches in Christ Jesus."

Reflection Questions

1. How are you personally doing at managing your money? Do you stick to a budget, or do you tend to overspend? Here's a great "Checklist for Trustworthy Spending" I found in June Hunt's *Counseling Through Your Bible Handbook:*

    • Is this purchase a true *need* or just a *desire*?

    • Do I have adequate funds to purchase this without using credit?

    • Have I compared the cost of competing products?

    • Have I prayed about this purchase?

    • Have I been patient in waiting on God's provision?

    • Do I have God's peace regarding this purchase?

    • Does this purchase conform to the purpose God has for me?

    • Is there agreement with my spouse about this purchase?[13]

2. As a couple, have you ever sat down to discuss your finances—your responsibilities individually and together? Do you have a budget? Are you in debt, and do you have a plan to pay back any creditors you owe?

3. What can you do today that will encourage the beginning of a financial dialogue with your husband? If this dialogue does not happen, what will be the outcome?

4. Take time now to reflect on your current method of money management. Are you being a good steward of what God has given to you? Would He be pleased with your current financial status? If not, what will you do in the next week to start making the necessary changes?

I'm not telling him about...

3 How I Want to Be Loved

Any man who can drive safely while kissing a pretty girl is simply not giving the kiss the attention it deserves.

ALBERT EINSTEIN

EVERY WOMAN DREAMS ABOUT the way she wants to be loved, and the images in our minds vary widely. Tender and intimate moments, relaxed walks, diamonds, a day shopping without the kids, pampering fit for a queen...Regardless of how varied our dreams may be, they almost always include the rapt attention of our lover. "Although women say they don't like for men to stare at their bodies, they melt when a man they might be interested in looks deeply into their eyes."[1]

Different Lenses

Part of the adventure (and the frustration) of relating to men is that love means different things to different people, and they show it in quite different ways. Gary Chapman's classic book *The Five Love Languages* identifies the most common ways people want to be loved: quality time, words of affirmation, gifts, acts of service, and physical touch. Our men may have very different love languages than we do, so we may misinterpret or discount the ways they show their affection.

> Love is, above all, the gift of oneself.
>
> JEAN ANOUILH

For example, a friend told me about an insight she had into her relationship with her husband. Her love language is gifts, but his is quality time. To show his love, he often invites her to go with him to exotic places like Dick's Sporting Goods, the hardware store, or the log home expo. For years, she didn't understand what he was saying by his offers, so she usually told him, "No, I'm doing something else right now." To her, anything else was more important than watching him pick out a new shotgun! Years into their relationship, she realized that asking her to join him was his way of showing affection, and she changed her plans.

But the misunderstanding wasn't a one-way street. All those years, she measured his love by the gifts he gave. By his own admission, his batting average was dismal. He told me, "In all these years of birthdays, Christmases, anniversaries, and Valentine's Days, I don't think I've given her more than two things she didn't take back to the store to exchange." Clearly, these two were missing each other. He learned that to communicate love, he had to put more mental energy into gift buying. He talked to his wife's best friend to ask her for suggestions, and with her direction, his gifts became big hits with her, and she felt loved.

The lenses through which we look at love are colored by many factors: our upbringing, our personality, our culture, and the wounds we've experienced. Recently, I asked a number of women how they define love, and their answers startled me. Sarah had been wrestling with a lifetime of abuse from her father and her ex-husband. Her definition of love was "the absence of pain." Beth has lived with an alcoholic husband for 11 years, and she's played the role of an enabler. When I asked her, she said, "I feel loved when he needs me—which is all the time." Anika is a high-ranking executive in a major corporation. I'm sure she has a tender side, but few people see it. In a moment of transparency, she explained that love means that "others do what I tell them to do—it's about my power and their compliance." (I bet she's fun—*not!*)

These ladies' definitions of love aren't unique. Countless others' concepts of love are shaped by the wounds they've experienced. Many of them simply don't have any idea what genuine love, or "non-possessive warmth," looks like.

Love and Respect

What does love actually look like to a man? Bestselling author, speaker, and consultant Shaunti Feldhahn conducted an extensive survey asking a sample of men and women to choose between two bad outcomes. She asked, "If you had

> I could never love where I could not respect.
> CHARLOTTE ELIZABETH AISSE

to choose, would you rather 'feel alone and unloved in the world' or 'feel inadequate and disrespected by everyone'?"

Surprisingly, 74 percent of the men said they would rather be "alone and unloved" than "feel inadequate and disrespected." But only 26 percent of the women choose inadequacy and disrespect as the worst of the two evils.

Chuck Cowan, codeveloper of the survey, warned that being loved and being respected mean the same thing to men. The men taking the survey actually complained about the nature of the instrument because they couldn't separate love from respect!

The survey revealed trouble in paradise. Sadly, 81 percent of the men agreed that "my wife or significant other doesn't *respect* me right now." But only 19 percent said "my wife or significant other doesn't *love* me right now." Although respect and love are very closely tied, the men in this poll apparently were suffering more from feeling disrespected than from feeling unloved. Feldhahn wrote, "Probably the most important revelation was the fact that husbands need—desperately *need*—to be respected and built up by their wives."[2]

The survey doesn't try to determine the origin of men's perceptions about love and respect. It may be a product of DNA, or it could be determined by male roles in our culture. The important issue for women isn't the cause; it's the reality of their men's views about love and life. Some authorities have questioned the methods used in Feldhahn's research, but altering the methods probably wouldn't significantly alter the finding: If a man feels disrespected, he will feel unloved.

Similarly, John Gottman, author of *Why Marriages Succeed or Fail*, worked with a multimillion-dollar research laboratory while researching for his book. He concluded that marriage success may be summed up with two very familiar words—*love* and *respect*.[3] To put it in simple terms, we women need to hear, "Honey, I love you so much," and we need to communicate to our men, "Darling, I am so proud of you, and I trust you completely."

New Skills

The insights we gain from Feldhahn's and Gottman's research can dramatically change the way we communicate with our men. We understand that what connects with them may be very different from what rings our bells, so we can be a bit more patient when they just don't get it. We won't learn

> Let men tremble to win the hand of woman, unless they win along with it the utmost passion of her heart.
>
> NATHANIEL HAWTHORNE

new skills in giving and receiving love, however, if we sit back and demand that our men meet our needs first and always. We might need to take some initiative to get things started. This makes perfect sense. The law of the harvest says that we reap what we sow, after we sow, and more than we sow. If we sow demands or distance, that's what we're going to get back—in spades! But if we sow kindness and affirmation, our men will (usually, but perhaps later than we'd like) bend over backward to demonstrate their love for us.

They may need a little help though. Dave Barry describes the challenge this way:

> Guys are simple…women are not simple and they always assume that men must be just as complicated as they are, only way more mysterious. The whole point is guys are not thinking much. They are just what they appear to be. Tragically.

Well, it doesn't have to remain tragic. A little communication can work wonders.

Most women crave tenderness and attention. How do I know if someone is paying attention to me? Eye contact is certainly part of it, but I'm not convinced she's tracking with me unless she asks second and third follow-up questions. That's what I want Tim to do when I'm talking to him. If I feel that he's not really listening, I can snap at him for being "so insensitive" or stomp off in a huff, or I can gently ask, "If this isn't a good time to talk, that's fine. Let me know when it works for you. There are some things I want us to talk about."

Now, I really have to watch my tone of voice and my body language to make sure I'm not pouting and stomping. When this incredibly rare (I wish!) event happens, I try to think and pray before I say a word to Tim about not listening so I can check my heart and my emotions. I need to make sure the look in my eyes matches the words coming out of my mouth.

We can learn to communicate our desires to our men more effectively. We don't need to require heavy-duty conversations. In an unguarded moment when they are really listening, we can simply say, "Honey, I really like it when you listen to me like this. It means a lot to me." Or if you can't find many positive moments to affirm just yet, you can tell him, "I like it when you stop what you're doing and give me eye contact when I'm talking to you about important things. You don't have to do that all the time, but sometimes, it tells me that you're really interested in what I say." (I used to reach over and turn his chin toward me. That didn't usually go over too well.) Open communication doesn't have to focus only on listening skills. We can tell our men what we like about every aspect of love, describe our particular love language, and share particulars about what makes us feel accepted and adored.

These new skills may seem foreign to some of us, but all we need to practice them is a little forethought and a dab of courage.

Fantasy Island

Let's be honest. We may be walking with God and wanting our lives to line up with His purposes, but we're real women living in a real world. Seeing Brad Pitt's or Hugh Jackman's hotness in a film just might enflame a second or two of fantasy in our minds. But for many women it's not about sneaking out in some cave for sex. Rather, most of us get caught up in the love story. We want to play Romeo and Juliet. You be the prince, and I'll be the princess. The dreams we had before we were married—the ones about the ideal husband and wedding-day bliss—pop into our minds once again.

And though fleeting moments of daydreaming probably won't ruin our marriages, we need to recognize the danger and get those images out of our minds as quickly as possible. Some of us don't even try to get rid of them. We live in a dream world of passionate romance and great sex, and our real-life husbands can't hold a candle to the men in our fantasies.

It's perfectly good and right to daydream about romantic encounters with our men. That's part of the planning process for building a good relationship. But when our minds focus on someone other than our husbands, or if we try to make them into someone they will never be, we're in danger of poisoning our relationships by means of comparisons. Paul wrote to the Corinthians about the importance of controlling our thoughts.

> Though we live in the world, we do not wage war as the world does. The weapons we fight with are not the weapons of the world. On the contrary, they have divine power to demolish strongholds. We demolish arguments and every pretension that sets itself up against the knowledge of God, and we take captive every thought to make it obedient to Christ (2 Corinthians 10:3-5).

Disappointment

I'm convinced that many couples don't enjoy giving and receiving love because they're so disappointed with one another. One day, she wakes up and realizes the man lying next to her isn't everything she had hoped for. Rather than accepting and being grateful for him as God's good gift, seeds of resentment germinate, especially when he isn't meeting all of her expectations. Sooner or later, if he continues to let her down, her mind may begin to drift to other partners, real or imagined. This invisible and unspoken barrier of disappointment and demands will do nothing but lead to more unmet expectations and further resentment. Until this barrier is identified and broken down, the couple drifts along with a superficial relationship, longing for love and respect but extending resentment instead. This is fertile soil for fantasies.

Covenant Marriage

The covenant of marriage isn't only between two people; it's a covenant between those individuals and God to accept His provision, thank Him for His gifts, and trust Him to use two flawed people to create something beautiful. We may wish our men were as handsome and loving as the make-believe men we see in movies or novels, but wishing for something else blocks real love. From time to time, all of us need to say to God, *Lord, show me how to do what's right so both of us feel loved and so we can honor You together.* I believe God delights in this prayer of honesty and faith.

What You Can Say to Him

Think back over the history of your relationship with your husband or boyfriend. Let me ask you a few questions:

When were the times you felt especially loved?

What was going on at that time?

What started it, and what ended that season of your relationship?

When were the times he felt deeply respected?

How did you show your respect to him during that time?

What difference did it make in his affection for you?

Most of us can remember some really good times in our relationships. Reflecting on the way we felt during those days and nights isn't too hard. But we need to dig a little deeper and think about how we treated our men during those good times. Somehow, our communication enflamed their love for us, and they were thrilled to show it. Those memories can be wonderful starting points for future conversations.

We need to grasp the power of the law of the harvest. The way we treat our men determines (in part at least) the way they treat us. We don't have any guarantees, and if the relationship is tragically flawed by deep, unresolved wounds, those need to be healed so that love can flow more freely. Take time to think about how you can complete these statements:

> I'm so proud of you because...
>
> I appreciate the way you...
>
> This is something I like about you:...

But we're not finished. When he communicates his love or when the two of you are able to talk about building the relationship, you can tell him: "I like it when you..." Be specific and be playful. Some of those things may be deep and heavy, but many of them are simple, light, and fun.

Make sure your communication about your desires and pleasures is specific and sincere. Men get confused when we give them global instructions. Break it down, explain the specifics, and give illustrations of what you're talking about. Don't expect him to grasp your deepest thoughts the way your best girlfriend does. He's not her! Help him by giving him handles on your innermost thoughts and the desires of your heart. And when you make your statements of affirmation and respect for him, don't open your mouth until you really mean the words you say. Men may seem dense, but they know when we're faking it, and they resent empty words. When we're insincere, they assume we're only trying to manipulate them, and they're often right.

Talking about love is no big deal for some couples because they already discuss matters of the heart all the time. They've resolved any lingering disappointment with each other, and their rock-solid commitment is a firm foundation for genuine affection and affirmation.

Many couples, though, have only fleeting moments when they give and receive love. They need to identify any barriers, or at least one of them (that would be the women: you and me) needs to take the initiative to resolve disappointments and sincerely communicate respect to the other. Some couples, however, live in the same house in an armed truce. They barely talk about anything significant because they've had so much anger and hurt in the past. These people are like two porcupines in a small box. They feel stuck every time the other person moves an inch!

When I talk to women in marriages like this, I assure them that God is a God of redemption. He can do miracles, but most often, the miracle begins in us. Remember what we said earlier—the only person you can change is you. As we find God's love and mercy, we gradually open our hearts to experience healing of the hurts we've endured. Then, over time, we begin to apply the principles in this chapter. Deep hurts take time to heal, and entrenched, painful patterns in a relationship don't change overnight—but we can change them.

Wherever your relationship is today, ask God for wisdom to communicate more effectively with the man in your life. When dialogue is open, amazing things can happen. You will learn how he perceives you and how he wants to be treated, and you'll have the opportunity to share your heart and your desires with him. Don't expect him to read your mind. That's not the way men operate. Get over it, change your expectations, and tell him how you want to be loved.

In the Word: Chapter Three Application

I talk to women and hear about couples who live in loveless marriages—relationships of convenience—where the love has died or possibly never really existed in any substantial way to begin with. These couples believe that their current situations are really as good as they will ever get, and they have no hope that anything will change. As we discussed earlier in this chapter, we know that men and women see and experience love through very different sets of lenses—not good and bad lenses, just different. However, sometimes we do need to clean our lenses.

The Meaning of Love

> Dear friends, let us love one another, for love comes from God. Everyone who loves has been born of God and knows God. Whoever does not love does not know God, because God is love. This is how God showed his love among us: He sent his one and only Son into the world that we might live through him. This is love: not that we loved God, but that he loved us and sent his Son as an atoning sacrifice for our sins. Dear friends, since God so loved us, we also ought to love one another. No one has ever seen God; but if we love one another, God lives in us and his love is made complete in us...God is love. Whoever lives in love lives in God, and God in him (1 John 4:7-12,16).

Compare this passage on love with the culture we live in today. It's a culture that is loveless, heartless, cold, and self-centered. I used to think that loveless people were fairly rare. Now, it seems that loveless-ness is the norm—a far too common reality in our day.

The apostle Paul understood these latter days, when the love of many has grown cold, and he warned Timothy specifically about the people who would characterize the spirit of these last days.

> Mark this: There will be terrible times in the last days. People will be lovers of themselves, lovers of money, boast-ful, proud, abusive, disobedient to their parents, ungrateful, unholy, without love, unforgiving, slanderous, without self-control, brutal, not lovers of the good, treacherous, rash, conceited, lovers of pleasure rather than lovers of God—having a form of godliness but denying its power. Have nothing to do with them.

> They are the kind who worm their way into homes
> and gain control over weak-willed women, who are loaded
> down with sins and are swayed by all kinds of evil desires,
> always learning but never able to acknowledge the truth
> (2 Timothy 3:1-7).

This passage is a clear definition of self-absorption and loveless-ness. But God is able to create and help stir a heart of love even in the loveless, just as He is able to make a saint out of a desperate and self-absorbed sinner. God can use you in this process. So here's how we show love to a loveless and difficult person.

> Love is patient, love is kind. It does not envy, it does not
> boast, it is not proud. It is not rude, it is not self-seeking,
> it is not easily angered, it keeps no record of wrongs. Love
> does not delight in evil but rejoices with the truth. It always
> protects, always trusts, always hopes, always perseveres.
> Love never fails (1 Corinthians 13:4-8).

This chapter—the characteristics of love in its purest form—is known as the Love Chapter. I have heard it quoted many times in weddings. It is from a letter like the one the apostle Paul wrote to Timothy, but this one is to the church in Corinth. The Corinthians were struggling with loving one another and truly understanding what God's love was all about. I want to take a moment now and examine each characteristic that Paul contrasts with love. Love is not...

- *Envious or boastful.* The believers in Corinth were jealous about each other's spiritual gifts, saying that some were more important than others. They also boasted that their leaders were superior to other church leaders in their time. Paul wanted them to see that they were all God's servants and parts of the body of Christ—all equally important to fulfilling God's plan. To boast is to think only of oneself, and to love is to think primarily of others.

- *Proud or rude.* Being arrogant means to esteem oneself too highly and as more valuable and important than others. Rudeness displays a lack of respect for other people. Where arrogance and rudeness are common, love is not present.

- *Self-seeking.* When I read this, I immediately think about a toddler who wants his own way, seeks attention, and demands immediate gratification. Love is not self-centered.

- *Angry and unwilling to let go of wrongs.* Love is not irritable or resentful—it does not hold grudges. If you love someone, you won't keep an ongoing record of what that person has done wrong or how he has offended you. This doesn't mean you will necessarily forget the issue or completely heal from the scar, but you can offer forgiveness.

- *Rejoicing in evil.* There is no room for pleasure in evil things. Loving believers will not seek to find fault in others but will recognize that no one is perfect—including themselves.

In addition to defining what love is *not*, Paul offers the most beautiful definition of what love *is:*

- *Patient and kind.* Love is not in a hurry.

- *Rejoices with the truth.* Love delights in the good things in life.

- *Always protects.* Love wants what's best for the other person even when that person is not so easy to love.

- *Always trusts, hopes, and perseveres.* Love is everlasting!

I am heartbroken when women tell me, "Julie, I thought we were in love when we were dating…I thought we were in love when we got married…I envisioned a 1 Corinthians 13 kind of love right from the start…but now it's different…things have changed." Always remember that love is a *choice.* Love is a *decision*—it is something that you *do.* Love requires action!

I respond gently by saying the only person you can change is you.

Begin to pray and ask for God's strength to love the man in your life—even during the difficult times. God can use your true and enduring love to help restore the relationship. Become a student of your husband. Learn to speak his love language. Start being the kind of loving person you would like him to be.

Please understand that I am not referring to becoming a doormat in the name of love, permitting him to use and abuse you. We will cover this issue in chapter 7. Enabling bad behavior and allowing abuse to continue is *not* true love. Sometimes love must be tough—but it's still love. Ask for God's wisdom and guidance. He will bless and use your desire to act out the love you have for the man in your life!

The Meaning of Respect

Scripture instructs husbands and wives to respect one another. But as we discussed in this chapter, the issue of respect means a lot more to the man in your life than you might have realized.

> "For this reason a man will leave his father and mother and be united to his wife, and the two will become one flesh." This is a profound mystery—but I am talking about Christ and the church. However, each one of you also must love his wife as he loves himself, and the wife must respect her husband (Ephesians 5:31-33).

At the start, we see a beautiful comparison of marriage to the love between Christ and His church. When a man and woman marry, they are joined together as one for a lifetime. In the same way, Jesus desires to become one with us as His children and believers. The marriage relationship is a tangible, daily reminder of God's everlasting companionship with His children.

Paul concludes this chapter by saying that above all, a husband is to love his wife and the wife is to respect her husband. Regardless of what our society may say about the role of the Christian wife regarding godly submission and respect, the Bible is clear and remains the final authority. We bring honor and glory to God by obeying Him.

It is also important to note that the command to respect is not an if-then statement. Paul did not say, "If your husband loves you, then you are to respect him." Scripture is very clear on this issue, and that's just the way it is. When you show respect to the man in your life, you fill his "love tank." And when he feels loved, he will want to give that love back to you!

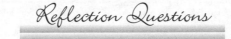

Reflection Questions

1. Do you know your love language? Do you know your man's love language? If not, make an effort to discover what each of your love languages is and whether you have been using the right languages.

2. Have you been withholding respect from your husband because you don't feel loved? Start thinking of simple ways you can show him respect throughout the day and then practice these techniques. Remember, by doing so, you are bringing honor to God, and He will bless you.

3. If you are feeling unloved, take a moment to rest in the Lord today. Go to His Word and see just how much He loves you. No man is ever going to love you perfectly, but God does! Find your satisfaction in Him first. Meditate on these Scriptures: 2 Corinthians 5:17; Ephesians 2:19; 1 Peter 2:9-10; 1 John 4:7-12.

I'm not telling him about...

4 How I Feel About Our Sex Life

Anybody who believes that the way to a man's heart is through his stomach flunked geography.

ROBERT BYRNE

HOW MANY OF US CAN RELATE to the restaurant scene in *When Harry Met Sally* when Sally faked an orgasm and the lady at the nearby table tells her waiter, "I'll have what she's having"? Most men have no idea how much sex—*meaningful* sex, that is—means to us, and they can't fathom the depths of our hopes and fears related to sexual performance. (I thought I might start this chapter with a little jolt.)

We live in a sex-saturated culture. Everywhere we look, we see seductive images and hear enticing words. Men and women may have differing hopes about sex, but it's one of the most powerful forces in human nature. Some couples talk openly about their desires, pleasure zones, creative positions, and problems related to their sex lives, but many couples talk with each other about anything and everything except their sex. Their partners have to guess what their desires might be, and they can only hope they connect enough emotionally and physically to make it worth the effort.

Maybe one or both of the partners feel ashamed about body image, past problems, or present performance. Or maybe they're insecure in the relationship, so they don't know how to interpret what sex really means. Instead of it being fulfilling and fun, it feels manipulative and empty. And some of us grew up in families where sex was simply never mentioned. Everybody knew it happened occasionally, but it was a taboo subject. Our silence about the subject is following the example of our parents, and we're modeling the same thing to our kids.

Sexual hopes and dreams are completely normal, and so are struggles in this area of our lives. In this chapter, I want to *demystify* sex by speaking the truth, and I want to *demagnify* it by sharing some ways you can talk to your husband about your sex life. During the sexual revolution, lots of people gravitated toward one of two extremes: Either sex was all they talked about or it was a taboo subject. We need a healthy balance. I'm no Dr. Ruth or Dr. Laura, but God has provided keen insights that can bring freedom into the bedroom.

Reality in the Bedroom

At our most recent Love for Life Conference held annually on Valentine's Day weekend, Dr. Kevin Leman spoke on the differences between men and women in the bedroom. As he spoke I laughed, realizing the humorous reality of what he was saying. When he spoke about when men and women most want sex, he said, "Men most desire sex in the mornings." Then he paused and asked, "And when do women most enjoy sex?" After a long, fun pause, he said, "June."

> Sex at the age of eighty-four is a wonderful experience. Especially the one in the winter.
> MILTON BERLE

A *Redbook* survey probed the intimate moments of women by asking them two questions: How often do you have sex? How often do you want to have sex? This simple research didn't dwell on the quality of orgasms or the creativity of positions. It focused only on quantity. Here's what they found:

How often do you have sex?		How often would you like to have sex?	
5% —	Once a day at least!	24% —	Every day.
25% —	Three to six times a week.	43% —	Three to six times a week.
35% —	Once or twice a week.	26%	Once or twice a week.
19% —	Two or three times a month.	5% —	Two or three times a month.
10% —	Once a month or less	2% —	Once a month or less.[1]

Do these numbers surprise you? Another *Redbook* article reports Michele Weiner Davis' research. She found that 60 percent of women said they were as interested or more interested in sex than their husbands were. Not surprisingly, the lower-desire partner determines the frequency of sex, but the gap between desire and reality bothers women far more than men. And though I'm not sure how confident I am in the representative sample of *Redbook* readers, the survey itself certainly gives us content to think about and breaks the traditional stereotype of the reluctant wife![2]

Interestingly, another study found that men prefer greater variety of sexual techniques, stimulation, and play, but women want consistency in the techniques and emotional connections through tenderness and intimate conversation.[3] These differences can be sources of misunderstanding, and if they aren't resolved, they can lead to serious conflict.

Many men and women harbor secret sexual fantasies they've never shared with anyone, even their spouses. They deeply desire more creativity and fulfillment in bed, but they're afraid to talk about their desires. But creative, stimulating sex isn't just for Hollywood stars or athletic young adults. According to Tim and Beverly LaHaye's "The Act of Marriage After 40 Survey," 47 percent of men "sometimes" manipulate their wife's clitoris orally, 48 percent of women enjoy it, and 41 percent of women "sometimes" use oral stimulation on their husbands. (The lady in your Bible study looking over your shoulder just gasped all the air out of the room.)

God's Plan for Sex

From the beginning, sex was God's idea, and He intended it to be one of the most fulfilling activities in a couple's relationship. The act of marriage is immensely pleasurable, and it cements the two individuals as "one flesh." Most churches don't talk much about sex, so many Christians

> Eros will have naked bodies; friendship, naked personalities.
> C.S. LEWIS

feel embarrassed by the subject. Because it's avoided, some women assume it's somehow not on the list of God's best gifts. But in fact, it's near the top! The Bible certainly has a lot to say about purity. One of the Ten Commandments forbids adultery, and in many passages we're warned about the damage inflicted by casual sex. Solomon spends much of the first nine chapters of Proverbs on the subject.

Tucked into the pages of our Bibles, we find an intriguing (and racy!) little book called Song of Solomon. For centuries, stuffy theologians haven't known what to do with this little book. It seems to describe passionate lovemaking, but surely, they concluded, God wouldn't put something like that in the Bible! But He did. Let's look at just a couple of excerpts.

In one passage, the lover paints a beautiful word picture of his wife's body. He describes her elegance, and he delights in "browsing among the lilies," which is a euphemism for intimate sexual exploration.

> Your lips are like a scarlet ribbon;
>   your mouth is lovely.
> Your temples behind your veil
>   are like the halves of a pomegranate.

Your neck is like the tower of David,
    built with elegance;
on it hang a thousand shields,
    all of them shields of warriors.
Your two breasts are like two fawns,
    like twin fawns of a gazelle
    that browse among the lilies.
Until the day breaks
    and the shadows flee,
I will go to the mountain of myrrh
    and to the hill of incense.
All beautiful you are, my darling;
    there is no flaw in you (Song of Solomon 4:3-7).

In another passage, the woman describes a particularly pleasurable moment lying in the arms of her lover. This pair isn't passive! She views him as a prancing gazelle, as handsome and strong as a young buck. And she says that he smells incredibly good, exciting her senses with fragrant spices.

His left arm is under my head
    and his right arm embraces me.
Daughters of Jerusalem, I charge you:
    Do not arouse or awaken love
        until it so desires...
You who dwell in the gardens
    with friends in attendance,
    let me hear your voice!
Come away, my lover,
    and be like a gazelle
    or like a young stag
    on the spice-laden mountains
        (Song of Solomon 8:3-4,13-14).

"Spice-laden mountains"? "Dwelling in the garden"? Can you believe this is in the Bible? I'm not so sure you'll find this in the video Bible study on Tuesday morning. But it is exciting. Many of us, though, endure repressed sexual urges and limited joy in bed. Author Linda Dillow observed, "Some women have spent so many years 'damming up' their sexual passions in an attempt to remain pure that they find it difficult to suddenly open the floodgates and allow sexual feelings to flow."

Don't be misled any longer into thinking that God's plan for you doesn't include sexual pleasures. The open, loving, and joyful expression of sexual desire in marriage is good and godly. The thrills we enjoy with our husbands fulfill our marriage vows to become one. God doesn't scowl at us when we plan creative sexual encounters with our husbands, and He doesn't frown when we actually enjoy ourselves. He delights in us enjoying the good gifts He has given us.

Common Struggles

But for some of us, all may not be well between the sheets. Recent research reports that 50 percent of women find sex to be either depressing, embarrassing, or a hassle. A significant number, 29 percent, say they're just too tired to be engaged in meaningful sex. Having children can erode sexual desire and opportunities. Women report that in addition to being exhausted from caring for their children all day, they're afraid their kids might walk in during lovemaking. In fact, more than a quarter of the women

> Some women have spent so many years "damming up" their sexual passions in an attempt to remain pure that they find it difficult to suddenly open the floodgates and allow sexual feelings to flow.
>
> LINDA DILLOW

surveyed said that their sex lives declined in meaning and frequency when they had children.[4]

Women may lose interest in sex for various reasons. One out of three women reports a decline in sexual desire at some point in her life. The risk of pregnancy causes some women to be more cautious. Men may feel free to engage in sex whenever they feel like it, but women intuitively know that joy for a moment might lead to a baby—along with a completely different lifestyle and a new weight of responsibility.

Certainly, the quality of a woman's relationship with her husband greatly affects her desire to jump into bed with him. He may be able to isolate relational conflicts and keep them outside the bedroom, but she can't! Tenderness, understanding, and patience are important for a woman to experience arousal, and those things are in short supply when resentment rules the home. Unfortunately, in such cases, the old traditional "quickie" to relieve him becomes the couple's standard for lovemaking, leaving her empty and feeling less loved.

Fluctuations in the level of hormones affect sexual desire. Breast-feeding and menopause can reduce a woman's passion. In addition, lower estrogen levels often result in vaginal dryness, making sex painful. Many authorities say that our hormones peak in our midtwenties and decline gradually until menopause, when they drop dramatically. Of course, emotional stresses, such as burnout and depression, dampen a woman's desire for sex, and some of the medications prescribed to treat these problems also have negative effects on libido.

For women, dramatic changes in lifestyle often have a negative impact on sexual desire. Having children, moving to another community, getting fired or laid off from a job, caring for aging parents, and any other major change can short-circuit passion and make sex less appealing.[5]

External stresses, however, are only part of the problem. Women who are overweight often avoid sex because they are ashamed of their bodies. A study of these married women found that 10 percent hadn't had sex in a year, and 70 percent said they do anything they can to avoid being seen naked by their partner. They've come up with some creative means to stay shrouded:

> pretending to have a headache
>
> having sex with the light off
>
> getting undressed before their husbands come to bed
>
> keeping a T-shirt or nightie on
>
> staying under the sheets and blankets

You know you're in trouble when he comes home on Valentine's Day and you're in an old, holey robe; your thick, nasty glasses are on; and your hair is up in a bun.

Take Care of Yourself

Sex and relationships expert Tracey Cox observes, "Sex is about what's happening on the inside, not how we look on the outside, but society definitely dictates that slim is attractive. So slimmer people do tend to feel more sexually confident."[6] Being overweight, though, often is a more complex issue than simply not knowing when to put the fork down. For many women, the stresses of life and feelings of loneliness seem overwhelming, and food is the most consistent form of comfort they can find. Still others feel so threatened by the risk of rejection in relationships that they subconsciously eat to gain weight. They want to look unattractive so people won't expect much of them. Being fat lowers the risk of intimacy.

What You Can Say to Him

Have you taken stock of your sex life as you've read this chapter? I'm sure you have. You probably can remember times when sex was thrilling and enjoyable. You can return to those feelings. You can be even better! You won't make much progress, though, without being honest with yourself and making a commitment to talk more openly with your husband about your desires and fears. As most sex experts would agree, great sex never starts in the bedroom. Communication and creativity are the spice of life between the sheets.

Men can be very defensive about their sexual prowess, so be careful how you begin a conversation about sex. You might want to open the dialogue by talking about a time when sex was really fun. Tell him how much you desire him (that'll turn him on and lower his defenses), and explain that you want this part of your relationship to be rich and meaningful for both of you. Don't point out any deficiencies on his part; talk only about your own hopes and desires. Remember, he thrives on feeling respected.

As the conversation continues, share any fear or discouragement you may have, and invite him to speak to your heart. Be sure to listen to him as he responds. If either of you becomes frustrated or defensive, don't let your emotions escalate. Stop the conversation by saying, "I'm sorry. This isn't what I meant to happen at all. I love you so much, and I want this part of our lives to be wonderful for both of us. Let's talk about this tomorrow."

Consider the factors that inhibit and enhance sexual pleasure, and talk about those with your husband. Some won't surprise him—he's well aware of the impact of lifestyle changes, financial pressures, and parenting challenges. But he may not know how or how much your changing hormones and other physiological issues affect you. Talking about these can bring understanding, and that's a wonderful environment for tenderness and intimacy.

Don't focus only on problems. Tell him what turns you on and gives you the most pleasure and what doesn't. He may think that sticking his tongue halfway down your throat is exciting. (You may be much less excited about not being able to breathe.) For many women, good lubrication covers a multitude of problems. Don't skimp on this simple solution. Keep a tube next to the bed, and be ready to use it.

Just having it handy helps some women relax and be more responsive to foreplay.

In many areas of life, predictability is a virtue, but in sex, it can be a killer. In fact, consider getting out of ruts in different parts of your life: cooking, television, hobbies, conversation topics, schedule, and especially your sex life.

In this book, I've warned against fantasizing about intimate relationships with other men, but I want to encourage you to daydream about great sex with your husband. This kind of fantasy is a good first step to a fresh approach to sex. Imagine intimate foreplay and creative sex at different times and places, and think about how you might entice him in ways you have never dreamed of. We can get so tired and our routine can become so mundane that all the spice of life is slowly squeezed out. Don't let that happen any longer. Change probably won't happen without a plan, and a spicy daydream might help you plan more effectively.

And when the time is right, like when both of you are aroused, give him details about what pleases you. Some husbands don't fully understand the enormous pleasure we find in the 8000 nerves of our clitoris—and all of these nerve endings are designed to give us maximum pleasure! Gentle stimulation can bring us ecstasy.

But clitoral stimulation isn't the only source of joy. In the 1950s, Dr. Ernest Grafenberg described a point in the anterior wall of a woman's vagina, named for him and called the "G-spot," that provides immense sexual pleasure. The paraurethral gland is located between the urethra and the vagina. Stimulation of the G-spot, generally takes longer than clitoral orgasms, but the effect can be even more powerful—so powerful, in fact, that not all women enjoy them. Many couples don't even know this point exists, but when they find it, the discovery can change their sex lives like nothing else.

> Just because you begin to experience a (G-spot) orgasm
> doesn't mean you have to stop! Although multiple orgasms

are far more difficult for men, women have the luxury of a much shorter refractory period, which means she can be an orgasmic Energizer bunny and keep going and going if she wants to. A woman's body is capable of experiencing these intense waves of pleasure over and over for several minutes (some report up to half an hour or more).[7]

Don't wait any longer. Open the dialogue with your husband today. My guess is that he'll feel thrilled and relieved that you brought up the subject. No—I am confident he will. He has probably wanted for a long time to talk about your sex life, but he didn't know how. Tell him how happy you are to be his, and tell him that you want your sex life together to be better than ever. A little steam and heat never hurt anyone!

In the Word: Chapter Four Application

I know what you're thinking. An application section in the sex chapter! If you have jumped to this section from a previous application section in the book, sorry—I couldn't work in the pictures!

Low-Sex, No-Sex Marriages

If you are married, let's start on common ground. We have all allowed the demands and pressures of life to rob us not only of some sexual experiences with our husband but also of some of our sexual desires. I know many men and women who are even tempted to label midlife as the sex-free stage of living. They settle for low-sex or no-sex marriages that have lost their passion and romance. Inhibited (or low) sexual desire, or ISD—also known as sexual aversion or hypoactive sexual desire—is increasingly common for people who invest themselves in just about everything except being sexual and satisfied. And this is not merely a female disorder—nearly as many men succumb to this problem as do their mates. Furthermore, the stresses and demands of life are not the only things that couples must think about and manage. We also have to account for the biology of our brains and the inevitable physiological, hormonal changes that affect sexual abilities and desires throughout our lives. And then there is the issue of our relationships themselves and how well we are nurturing them.

I want to talk briefly about low-sex, no-sex marriages by starting with biblical instructions regarding sex, and I'll follow that up with a more clinical review of the problem and what to do about it.

Biblical Directions

Paul directly addresses the issue of sex. "Do not deprive each other except by mutual consent and for a time, so that you may devote yourselves to prayer. Then come together again so that Satan will not tempt you because of your lack of self-control" (1 Corinthians 7:5). When we further add Proverbs 5:15,18-19, the picture of God's intent for us is completed: "Drink water from your own cistern, running water from your own well…May your fountain be blessed, and may you rejoice in the wife of your youth. A loving doe, a graceful deer—may her breasts satisfy you always, may you be ever captivated by her love."

These passages clearly instruct couples not to deprive one another sexually. Sex is best seen as an appetite and a mutual responsibility. Do not give in to and become a slave to the feelings of a low-sex, no-sex marriage, even when those feelings include exhaustion and lack of attraction to your mate. If you do, refrain only by mutual consent for the purposes of seeking greater intimacy with God. The writers of the Bible recognize that sex is a drive that needs its continuing place in marriage. Therefore if we are allowing anything other than communion with God to interfere with consistent (and not necessarily frequent) sex, we have crossed a line that is hurting us and our marriage, and one that will tempt us to do greater wrong if we continue.

The Bible also directly addresses sexual immorality. When you are hungry and your stomach is empty, what do you do? You go looking for food, right? The same is true regarding sexual gratification. If the sex appetite is not fulfilled, the temptation to go looking for fulfillment is strong. Hebrews 13:4 says, "Marriage should be honored by all, and the marriage bed kept pure, for God will judge the adulterer and all the sexually immoral." Paul gives the Corinthians this reminder:

> Flee from sexual immorality. All other sins a man commits are outside his body, but he who sins sexually sins against his own body. Do you not know that your body is a temple of the Holy Spirit, who is in you, whom you have received from God? You are not your own; you were bought at a price. Therefore honor God with your body (1 Corinthians 6:18-20).

But even though sex can be compared to the appetite for food, it is so much more! The Corinthians believed sex was *only* about filling an appetite and no different from the need for food. Paul warned against this kind of viewpoint: "'Food for the stomach and the stomach for food'—but God will destroy them both. The body is not meant for sexual immorality, but for the Lord, and the Lord for the body" (1 Corinthians 6:13).

Physical intimacy is about the coming together of two bodies and two souls for the purpose of gratification and celebration of a union ordained and blessed by God. It is two people honoring the Lord with their bodies by intimately joining their flesh and spirit in the bond of pure love and desire. When this happens, the husband and wife are sexually satisfied, and God is glorified!

A Counseling Definition

ISD simply refers to a low level of sexual interest. A person with ISD will not instigate sexual activity or respond to the spouse's desire for it. ISD can be primary (the person has never felt much sexual desire or interest) or secondary (the person used to feel sexual desire but no longer does). ISD can also relate only to the spouse, bringing the risk of infidelity (the person with ISD is interested in other people but not his or her spouse), or it can be general (the person with ISD isn't sexually interested in anyone). In the extreme form of sexual aversion, the person not only lacks sexual desire but also may find sex disgusting and repulsive.

Sometimes, the sexual desire is not inhibited. The two partners may have different sexual interest levels even though both of their interest levels are within the normal range. Someone can claim that his or her partner has an inhibited sexual disorder when in fact the first person has overactive sexual desire and is sexually demanding.

Causes and Risk Factors

ISD is a common sexual disorder. Often it occurs when one partner does not feel intimate or close to the other. Communication problems, lack of affection, power struggles and conflicts, external and chronic stressors, and not having enough time alone together are common factors. ISD can also occur in people who have had a very strict upbringing concerning sex, people who have learned negative attitudes toward sex, and people who have been victims of traumatic sexual experiences (such as rape, incest, or any other sexual abuse).

Illnesses and various medications are also contributors, especially when they cause fatigue, pain, or general feelings of despair. A lack of certain hormones can sometimes be involved. Psychological conditions such as anxiety, depression, and excess stress can dampen sexual interest. Hormonal changes can also affect libido. Commonly overlooked factors include insomnia or lack of sleep, which lead to fatigue. ISD can also be associated with other sexual problems and sometimes can be caused by them. For example, the woman who is unable to have an orgasm or has pain with intercourse and the man who has erection problems (impotence) or retarded ejaculation can lose interest in sex because they associate it with loss or failure, or because sex no longer feels pleasurable.

Solutions or Treatment

Treatment must be targeted to the factors that may be lowering sexual interest. Some couples will need relationship or marital therapy before focusing on enhancing sexual activity. Some couples will need to be taught how to resolve conflicts and work through differences in nonsexual areas. Communication training helps couples learn how to talk to one another, show empathy, resolve differences with sensitivity, and respect each other's feelings. Couples may also need to learn how to express anger in positive ways, reserve time for activities together, and show affection in order to encourage sexual desire.

Many couples will also need to focus on their sexual relationship. Through education and assignments for couples, they can learn to increase the time they devote to sexual activity. Some will need to focus on how they can sexually approach each other in more interesting and desirable ways as well as how to gently and tactfully decline a sexual invitation.

If couples have problems with sexual arousal or performance that affect their sexual drive, they will need to address these issues directly. Some doctors recommend treating women with either cream or oral testosterone, often combined with estrogen, but no clear-cut evidence has yet proven this to be effective. Studies are underway to determine the possible benefit of testosterone supplementation for women with decreased libido.

Disorders of sexual desire are often difficult to treat. They seem to be even more challenging to treat in men. For help, get a referral to someone who specializes in sex and marital therapy.

Becoming Sexual Again

When both partners have low sexual desire, sexual interest level may not cause problems in the relationship. On the other hand, low sexual desire may be a sign of an unhealthy relationship. In an excellent and loving relationship, low sexual desire may cause a partner to feel hurt and rejected. This can lead to feelings of resentment and make partners feel emotionally distant. Sex can either bring a couple closer together or slowly drive them apart. When one partner is much less interested in sex than the other partner, and this has become a source of conflict, they should get professional help before the relationship becomes further strained.

One good way to overcome and prevent ISD is to set aside time for nonsexual intimacy. Couples who reserve time each week for talking and for a date alone without the kids will keep a closer relationship and are more likely to feel sexual interest. Couples should also separate sex and affection so that they won't be afraid that affection will always be seen as an invitation to have sex. Reading books or taking courses in communication for couples or massage can also encourage feelings of closeness.

Regularly setting aside "prime time" (before exhaustion sets in) for talking and for sexual intimacy will improve closeness and sexual desire. Midlife couples and seniors must proactively schedule time for sexual and other intimacies. Couples with high levels of responsibility must make this a priority, or other things will always rise up and interfere.

Reflection Questions

1. Is talking about sex with your husband difficult? If you are single, do you know your boyfriend's viewpoint regarding sex in marriage? What are your personal barriers to discussing this issue?

2. On a scale of one to ten, with one being very low and ten being very high, what is your current level of sexual desire? How can you move up on that scale?

3. Do you ever initiate sex with your husband? If not, do you think this would help improve your relationship?

4. Take a moment to pray and ask God to show you areas of your sexual relationship with your husband that could be better. Ask Him to give you the strength and willingness to address these issues and make the necessary changes. Then schedule a time with your husband to talk about what God has revealed to you.

I'm not telling him about...

5 My Past: Secrets and Private Issues

*Your past is not your past
if it's affecting your present.*

A FRIEND OF MINE ASKED HER SISTER, "What's the one thing you *never* want your husband to know about you?" Yikes!

Maybe your life is all in order, and you don't have any deep, dark secrets. But a lot of women do. Or maybe you don't think about those private issues all the time, but at certain moments, an old photo album, particular smells, or an old song on the radio brings up images from the deep well of your memories. American novelist and children's writer Alice Hoffman commented, "I think secrets often come out. I spoke to a friend who is a therapist and I asked her if there were people who came to her and admitted to doing horrible things and she said, 'More than you know.'" Some of those horrible things are sins we've committed that hurt God, ourselves, or people we love, and some are horrible things people have done to us.

When They Remain Hidden

As long as we try to keep these unresolved or painful ghosts in the closet, they retain their power over us. Have you ever thought about how many scenes in horror movies are set at night? Our haunting memories feed on our secret fears, and they multiply our sense of dread. The fear of rejection is pretty standard for all of us, but people with ghosts from the past often live with the paradoxical fears of not being known (because they know they're not open and honest about their secrets) and the fear of being exposed (if someone knew the truth). Can you relate to that paradox? I hope not, but many of us can identify with it very easily.

I'll never forget innocently meeting up with a high school flame while I was dating Tim. I had returned to Montana to live with my parents during a break from college, and I decided to go skating with some friends. That evening, I ran into the former boyfriend. Tim, who was still back in Virginia, lived with my parents during our breaks from college and was scheduled to arrive in Montana a few weeks after me. I didn't see any reason to mention my roller rink rendezvous with the old squeeze—until the rascal started calling me!

Tim, who had since arrived at my parents, was getting suspicious, wondering who was calling me and why. I was "skating" again, but this time it wasn't fun. I skated around the issue too long without telling Tim the truth. Then it ended. High school Harry called me one day when Tim was standing not too far from me. After asking who it was, Tim asked to say hello to him. Well, that was fun. Needless to say, that was the end of the drama with the third wheel. But Tim and I suffered a break in trust for a little while.

When the Past Meets Your Present

Too many women have suffered for years under a cloud of regret, guilt, and shame for things they did decades ago, and many others have lived with bitterness against someone who hurt them. A lot of women feel overwhelmed by a lethal combination of shame and bitterness. The events that caused these consuming feelings may have occurred long ago, but they can affect every decision and relationship today.

> I've never tried to block out the memories of the past, even though some are painful. I don't understand people who hide from their past. Everything you live through helps to make you the person you are now.
>
> SOPHIA LOREN

Susan asked to talk to me after I spoke at one of our conferences. She had a sweet smile, but I could tell something was bothering her. We went to a restaurant, and I asked for a booth in the back where we could talk in private. I sensed she needed to talk about something really significant. After a few minutes of getting acquainted, a tear began to roll down her cheek as she said, "Julie, I can't live with it anymore." For the next 20 minutes, she told me about the anguish she had endured for 27 years.

When she was in high school, she dated one of the football stars. They had sex several times, and she got pregnant. She was terrified, and she felt she couldn't tell her parents about it—especially her father. A close friend took her to a doctor who performed a backroom abortion. That, she hoped, would be the end of it. But it wasn't—not by a long shot.

When she began dating Phillip, she never mentioned a word about her previous pregnancy and abortion. For all he knew, she was a virgin on their wedding night. She told me, "We have three beautiful children, and by all accounts, a happy marriage." She took a deep breath and then said, "I've tried so hard to put it out of my mind, but I just can't. I think about that dear child almost every day. Whenever I hear babies crying, I feel as if I'm going crazy." She took a second to gather herself. "Julie, can you help me? I don't know where else to turn."

I asked, "Have you thought about telling Phillip?"

Susan looked forlorn and instantly replied, "About a million times."
"Why didn't you? Do you think he'd be angry?"

She sighed, "When we were first married, I didn't want to spoil his image of me. Then as the years passed, I realized that if I told him, he'd have every right to wonder why I'd kept it a secret. I was afraid for one reason long ago, and for another reason since then. Either way, I've kept it a secret."

I asked, "How do you think it's affected your relationship?"

She shook her hair back, gathered herself, and fought back a tear. "I don't know. He's so kind to me, but there's always a bit of suspicion in my heart. I wonder how he'd respond if he knew. I think he'd be okay with it. He'd probably forgive me, but I have this nagging little doubt. I can hear him in my mind calling me a baby killer. I think that's affected how much I trust him." Her eyes suddenly flashed with insight, and then she told me, "I know it sounds ridiculous that *I don't trust him*. It's me, not him."

Susan's relationship with Phillip had been tainted by a secret sin. Let's look at the power of secrets, both sins and wounds.

The Downside

A secret can be as seemingly insignificant as hiding the extra money spent on some must-have new shoes or as important as maintaining a cover-up for a dishonest child. Other secrets may include privately carrying the weight of drug abuse, hiding some other addiction, or allowing undiscussed issues such as abuse to adversely affect the marriage.

> We cannot change our past. We cannot change the fact that people act in a certain way. We cannot change the inevitable. The only thing we can do is play on the one string we have, and that is our attitude.
>
> CHUCK SWINDOLL

Secrets are usually maintained for two key reasons—fear and shame. Fear includes the sense that something bad could happen as a result of disclosure of a secret. Shame includes the ongoing embarrassment and unresolved guilt that result from a secret. However, failure to disclose a secret will result in a double bind—a lose-lose type of proposition. If I do disclose, I may bring irreparable harm to my marriage. But if I don't disclose, I will never resolve the guilt and shame I am carrying— and surely this will erode the marriage over time. The end result leaves the secret keeper confused, fearful, and walking on a tightrope.

Private Issues

In my conversations about secrets with women across the country, they have mentioned a wide variety of issues that still haunt them. Three, though, stand out: abortions, sexual promiscuity, and walking away from people they love.

According to the Guttmacher Institute, 43 percent of American women have had an abortion. That stunned me the first time I read it. In many cases, the shock of being pregnant clouded their decision making. A day, a week, a month, or a year later, they began to struggle with what they did. Most of these women were single when they had abortions, but some were married. For some women, a bad marriage and financial pressures of adding another mouth to feed looked too daunting. Some didn't even tell their husbands they were pregnant. One study reports that nearly half of all pregnancies in America aren't intended, and of those that aren't wanted, 40 percent end in abortions.[1]

Another survey of women in post-abortion support groups revealed these statistics:

- 70 percent had a prior negative moral view of abortion.
- 30 to 60 percent wanted to keep their babies.
- More than 80 percent would have carried to term with better circumstances or more support of loved ones.

- 53 percent felt forced to have the abortion by people in their lives.

- 64 percent felt forced to have the abortion by circumstances in their lives.

- Almost 40 percent were still hoping to learn of some alternative to abortion when they sat down for counseling at the abortion clinic.[2]

Today, more and more women are seeking counseling to resolve the guilt they feel because of abortions that occurred many years before. I bring this up not to open an old wound, but to help you understand that you don't have to live in silence and shame any longer. God does forgive and bring healing to post-abortive women.

Past sexual promiscuity is an even more common challenge that haunts women. For many, the fact that "everybody was doing it" may temporarily ease some of the pangs of guilt, but those painful thoughts and feelings come up again and again. The Guttmacher Institute reports that by age 15, only 13 percent of teens have ever had sex. However, by the time they reach age 19, seven in ten teens have engaged in sexual intercourse. Today, parents of junior high school students must be concerned about their children's sexual experiments. The rapid explosion of sexually transmitted diseases is a huge problem. An estimated four million 12- to 17-year-olds will contract an STD this year alone.

The guilt, the concern about God's forgiveness, and the resulting effects of promiscuity cut deeply. Some of the women I've met had affairs while they were married. They initially tried to justify them because their husbands weren't emotionally available, and since then, they've tried to excuse the affairs by imagining that they weren't big deals. But their haunted memories reveal that the affairs *are* big deals. I found this statistic quite interesting: Affairs aren't only for the young. One study shows that extramarital affairs occur in 13 percent of couples who are 18 to 29 years old. The number rises to 20 percent for those in their forties. The figure declines to 9.5 percent for those who are 70 and older (which brings up other questions I don't even want to think about!).[3]

In addition to abortions and promiscuity, our broken relationships with those we love can cause painful memories that we try to hide. I've talked with scores of women who are heartbroken because they don't have relationships with their parents, siblings, or children. In almost all cases, everybody had a hand in the breakup, but these women recognize their part—they can't blame it all on the other people. And they hurt, usually alone and in silence. They vividly recall vicious arguments over major or petty grievances. Instead of seeking understanding and reconciliation, they stiffened their necks, demanded compliance, and either drove people away or walked out. Now they feel terrible about what they did, the pain they inflicted on others, and the deep grief they feel over lost love.

Natalie told me about the break in her relationship with her parents. Now 45 years old, she recounted the history of the problem. "I guess I was typical of most adolescents—headstrong, selfish, fiercely independent—but really, more that way than most. I partied a lot in college, smoked weed, and enjoyed myself. My parents, especially my dad, confronted me about my lifestyle. I blew them off, and they threatened to cut off funding for school. That really made me mad, and I called their bluff. I refused to change. I wouldn't even try to see things from their point of view. Finally, after pleading with me many times, Dad realized I wasn't going to budge an inch. He told me he wasn't paying for anything else until I changed my ways. For months, he and Mom thought I'd come around, but I didn't. I found a way to stay in school for a semester, but after that, I dropped out." She hesitated a moment and then continued. "But that's not the worst of it. I hated them for being so stubborn and selfish. The few times I visited them, we instantly got into huge fights with yelling and screaming—well, at least I was yelling and screaming. After a few of those, I walked out and never went back."

I asked, "What's your relationship been like for all these years?"

"Strained...distant...nonexistent," she lamented. "My husband and I have teenagers now, and he told me that it would be perfect justice if they rebel against us the way I rebelled against my parents. I sure don't want that to happen, but the first signs are already there."

"So," I asked, "have you and your husband talked about the problem with your parents?"

"Not really," she confided. "He's offered to talk about it, but it's too painful for me. I just keep thinking it's so far in the past that it can't affect me now. I guess all the regret is a sign I haven't dealt with it yet, huh?"

These are just snapshots of a few women who feel haunted from their past. We could list and describe countless other issues and scenarios. The point is that our refusal to talk about these things from the past can seriously erode our most cherished relationships today.

Secret Wounds

Novelist Walter J. Williams revealed, "I'm not afraid of werewolves or vampires or haunted hotels; I'm afraid of what real human beings do to other real human beings." Many women *feel* like victims precisely because they *are* victims. People they trusted used them, abused them, and hurt them terribly. Whether it happened once or a million times, the wounds caused by the sexual, physical, verbal, and emotional abuse don't heal quickly or easily. Many women have learned to live with deep gashes in their souls, but they don't live well. They limp through life with nagging pain and persistent bitterness at the ones who inflicted the pain. Those traumatic events may have occurred many years ago, but the victims look at every event today through the lenses of those past events.

People who live with unresolved wounds can easily take another path and become defensive and demanding. They resent anyone who gets in their way over any issue, and they expect others to jump in and fix their problems. They demand that the people who hurt them pay dearly for the wrong. This desire may begin with a sense of justice, and it can soon fester into a desire for revenge. They also demand that other people fill up the gaping holes created by the perpetrators. Of course, they don't tell these people they have such unrealistic expectations of them. When the other people fail to deliver, the victims discard them and try to find others to salve their wounds.

But there's more. Women who see themselves as victims can also indirectly demand that nobody ever hurt them again. They believe they've suffered enough, so no one better ever, under any circumstances, let them down.

Can you imagine how these demands color our relationships, especially with men? If we've been wounded in the past but we haven't resolved the pain, we'll expect our men to know, understand, and fix every problem, mend every hurt, and never ever fail us—even when they don't have a clue about what's going on inside of us. This is a recipe for more brokenness.

Tell Everything?

> What you are as a single person, you will be as a married person, only to a greater degree. Any negative character trait will be intensified in a marriage relationship because you will feel free to let your guard down— that person has committed himself to you, and you no longer have to worry about scaring him off.
>
> JOSH MCDOWELL

Couples often ask, "Is it really necessary to go back and drag out all of our dirty laundry and discuss in every detail our past?" Here are several guidelines we have found helpful:

First, remember that honesty must always take first place in your marriage. Although Scripture doesn't speak directly about keeping secrets specifically in marriage, it speaks plainly and often regarding secrets, honesty, and dishonesty in every relationship (Psalm 19:12; 90:8; Proverbs 27:5; Romans 2:16; Ephesians 4:25). Honesty is absolutely essential if our personal lives and marriages are to mature. And when a husband and wife commit to trust each other unwaveringly, they must respond to each other's personal issues (past and present) with grace, kindness, and love. A healthy marriage leaves no room for fear, chaos, and suspicion.

Second, keep in mind that we don't know or remember everything precisely, including the past and present events that we keep secrets about. Therefore, you probably won't be able to recall every detail of your secret. But that's okay—you do not have to know everything for love to grow and trust to flourish in your marriage.

Third, you must ask yourself an important question. Is the information you are withholding harmful to the marital bond? If the secret has the potential to cause damage, or if it is in any way keeping your intimacy from deepening and your love from growing, it needs to be disclosed.

Finally, do not get hung up on the past. If the secret is in the past—if it has been forgiven and resolved and is not relevant to or helpful in the present, disclosing it is not necessarily important. Let it be done. Let sleeping dogs lie! A selfish desire to attain information about a spouse's forgiven past can cause more pain than healing.

How to Disclose

If you have a troubling secret to disclose, what should you do? Seek outside help. Bring in a third party who can guide you and help you keep the marital bond strong. Pray individually and as a couple for God's protection on your relationship.

Before we decide what to say to the men in our lives, we first need to bring our sins and wounds into the light of God's grace. The Scriptures speak powerfully and eloquently about God's wonderful forgiveness. We don't have to live under the wet blanket of guilt and shame any longer. God offers cleansing, if we'll only accept it. King David knew this.

> He does not treat us as our sins deserve
>   or repay us according to our iniquities.
> For as high as the heavens are above the earth,
>   so great is his love for those who fear him;
> as far as the east is from the west,
>   so far has he removed our transgressions from us
>   (Psalm 103:10-12).

God never excuses sin, and He doesn't necessarily minimize the damage we've caused. Over and over again in the Gospels, we see Jesus looking sinners in the eye, speaking truth about their condition, and offering His gracious forgiveness. I love the account of the woman caught in adultery. (I know it's not included in the oldest and best manuscripts, but the story likely reflects something that really happened.) The Law commanded the community to stone her to death, but Jesus expressed His compassion and grace to her. He extends the same grace to us. Think about it this way: The sin we cover, God uncovers; the sin we uncover, God covers.

The early church wasn't much different from us. Paul's letters to the Christians in Corinth show that they struggled with sexual sins and selfishness. In his second letter to them, Paul refers to an earlier communication in which he boldly encouraged them to face their sins and turn to God. They responded to his exhortation, so he replied by affirming their faith:

> Even if I caused you sorrow by my letter, I do not regret it. Though I did regret it—I see that my letter hurt you, but only for a little while—yet now I am happy, not because you were made sorry, but because your sorrow led you to repentance. For you became sorrowful as God intended and so were not harmed in any way by us. Godly sorrow brings

repentance that leads to salvation and leaves no regret, but worldly sorrow brings death (2 Corinthians 7:8-10).

Do you see the difference between godly sorrow and worldly sorrow? Godly sorrow is the conviction of the Holy Spirit, who shines His light on our sins and offers God's forgiveness. Paul didn't tell the Corinthians their sin didn't matter, and he didn't try to explain it away. He called it sin. When God's Spirit points to sin we've committed, we feel remorseful, but we're deeply grateful for God's cleansing love. In stark contrast, worldly sorrow is just feeling rotten about what we've done and who we are. We don't feel worthy of being forgiven, so we wallow in self-pity. We may hope feeling bad enough long enough will make the awful feelings go away, but it doesn't. Penance isn't the same thing as genuine forgiveness. Worldly sorrow is a sense of shame that actually blocks our experience of God's forgiveness.

For some women, self-pity isn't a temporary problem; it's a lifestyle. Unresolved hurts can fester in our hearts. Over time, a core of resentment takes root, and we see ourselves only as "the one who was wronged." Soon, this resentment leads to self-pity, and we insist that we deserve better than we've gotten and that we're getting—from God, our families, our bosses, our children, and our friends. Self-pity may be a natural response to unhealed wounds, but it's deadly. It short-circuits our faith and makes us passive. Unless we address this pervasive spiritual problem, it will poison every relationship in our lives.

When we wallow in self-pity, we want attention, and we expect other people to fix our problems. We complain and moan, waiting for others to notice us and come to our rescue. When no one does, we have something else to moan about! Pastor John Piper, author of *Desiring God,* offers insight about the relationship of pride to self-pity:

> The nature and depth of human pride are illuminated by
> comparing boasting to self-pity. Both are manifestations
> of pride. Boasting is the response of pride to success. Self-
> pity is the response of pride to suffering. Boasting says,

"I deserve admiration because I have achieved so much."
Self-pity says, "I deserve admiration because I have sacri-
ficed so much." Boasting is the voice of pride in the heart
of the strong. Self-pity is the voice of pride in the heart of
the weak. Boasting sounds self-sufficient. Self-pity sounds
self-sacrificing. The reason self-pity does not look like pride
is that it appears to be needy. But the need arises from
a wounded ego, and the desire of the self-pitying is not
really for others to see them as helpless, but as heroes. The
need self-pity feels does not come from a sense of unwor-
thiness, but from a sense of unrecognized worthiness. It
is the response of unapplauded pride.[4]

I've seen self-pity block the flow of God's Spirit in countless wom-
en's lives. Certainly, many (if not all) of these women are victims of
others' sins against them, but nobody is perfect, and many of these
women become so defensive that they can't or won't admit their own
sin. They resist the Spirit's convicting presence, and they insist whatever they've done can't compare to what was done to them. Godly
sorrow? Not on your life! They feel much more comfortable—and self-
righteous—blaming others instead of taking responsibility for their
own sins and mistakes. When we make excuses for our behavior, we
miss out on the wonderful, cleansing love of Christ. Some of us need
tremendous courage to face the hard truth and admit that even when
we're victims, we too have need of repentance.

A friend of mine, Judith, told me about her struggles with self-pity.
She grew up in an alcoholic home. Her mother came home drunk
almost every night and either passed out or verbally assaulted everyone in the house. To her knowledge, her father never confronted his
wife or protected the children from her abuse. Whenever Judith and
her dad talked about her mom, which was very seldom, her dad just
shook his head and mumbled, "Blessed are the peacemakers. Honey,
that's my role, to be a peacemaker. I don't want to make your mother

any angrier than she already is." So the abuse, confusion, and hurt continued throughout Judith's childhood.

Psychologists describe a condition in victims' lives called "learned helplessness." It means that the persistently unhealthy environment causes people to give up hope that things can ever change, even when opportunities for change present themselves. Learned helplessness locks a person into the role of a victim. Judith told me that she married a man who was just like her mother—an abusive alcoholic. She divorced him, but a year later she married another alcoholic.

The daily stress and her sense of helplessness finally caused her to collapse mentally, emotionally, and physically. She became clinically depressed. In counseling, she learned some truths about the patterns of life and thinking that had kept her prisoner for so long, and she finally understood how learned helplessness had chained her to a destructive lifestyle. With the help of her counselor, a support group, a fresh set of eyes looking at God's Word, and the power of God's Spirit, she began to take steps out of the swamp of helplessness and despair. Slowly, she began to rebuild her life based on truth and grace. And gradually, she was able to be honest about her part in her problems. She admitted that she had chosen to believe lies, she had hurt others along the way, she had lied to cover up her pain and her husbands' behavior, and she had turned her back on God countless times. Her honesty led her to the cleansing flood of God's grace, and she found joy, love, and freedom for the first time in her life.

People who see themselves as victims aren't good at forgiveness— accepting it or extending it—because they blame others for every problem in their lives. And forgiveness starts with us. We need to experience God's grace before we can extend it to others. With honesty, amazing things are possible. Without it, we stay stuck in the smelly, slimy bog of thinking, feeling, and acting like helpless victims.

Regardless of what we've done and how badly we've blown it, the single most powerful message of the Bible is that none of us is beyond the reach of God's forgiving touch. Over and over again, the writers convince us that God's love is boundless and free. We need only to reach out and embrace it.

The Process of Forgiveness

To experience God's healing for wounds inflicted on us, we also need to grasp God's forgiveness. But in this case, we grasp it so we can extend it to those who hurt us. Grief and forgiveness are essential elements of healing. We grieve because we've lost something dear to us: our innocence, our dreams of being loved, or something else we treasured. The

> He who is devoid of the power to forgive, is devoid of the power to love.
> MARTIN LUTHER KING JR.

process of resolving our pain doesn't happen quickly, and it isn't neat and tidy. Grief is hard work, but it is essential if we're going to move past our pain. As we grieve, we are usually able to be increasingly honest about the people who hurt us. Before, we may have excused them or minimized the pain, but not any longer. As we face the hard facts of the hurt, we choose to forgive. Sooner or later, our feelings will catch up to our choices, but for now, we steadfastly choose to forgive, just as God in Christ has forgiven us.

What You Can Say to Him

If you've kept a secret from your husband or boyfriend for many years, your reluctance to talk to him probably reveals a high level of fear about how he might respond. In many cases, those fears are unfounded. I've talked to many women who finally told their men their deepest, darkest secrets, and their men showered them with understanding and love.

But of course, that's not always the case. I recommend that you first find a counselor, pastor, or exceptionally wise friend who can help you process the sin or wound and determine how to proceed. Be careful though. Some authorities counsel people to tell everything, regardless of the cost. Complete honesty, they assure us, is the only way to live. Others are more cautious and recommend that we avoid telling people things that will cause irreparable damage to the relationship. For example, confessing past sexual indiscretions may or may not be wise. The person who counsels you can give you advice about how to enter the conversation, how to explain yourself, how many details to share, what response to ask for, and how to build a healthier relationship with your man after you tell him your secret.

Our men may not be the most perceptive creatures God has created, but many of them can tell when some kind of barrier stands between them and us. They may think it's "just a female thing" that is totally unfathomable to them, but they may suspect that we're not willing to talk about something in our past. Maybe they've invited us to talk in the past, maybe not. They may, however, have more insight into us than we think.

If you determine that you want to talk to your man about your secret, prepare yourself for the conversation. Write down your goals for the talk and outline exactly what you want to say. Some women write out their statement and read it. That's not a bad idea. It enables them to stay on track, and it gives them confidence that they won't go brain dead in the middle of the conversation.

As you envision the talk, don't become fixed on a single way you want him to respond. If you've been uptight about this for years, it has surely become a big deal in the relationship. You can reasonably assume that he may need some time to grasp it, so don't demand that he instantly understand you perfectly. In fact, it would be wise to say something like this: "I know this is new to you, and I don't expect you to understand all the details and implications right away. We'll probably need to have several conversations about it."

Don't expect to be completely comfortable and at peace when you finally tell him. The fears you have felt for years will probably intensify in the moments before you say, "Honey, I want to tell you something."

Don't wait until fearful feelings evaporate; that's not going to happen. Be prepared and anticipate the feelings you'll have so you won't be surprised. If you're convinced that you're doing the right thing, press through your fears and begin this important dialogue.

He'll sense that you're nervous, so begin by saying, "There are some things I've never told you. I've wanted to, but I've been afraid. When I tell you, I think you'll understand why I've been hesitant. The problem, though, isn't you. It's me. You are trustworthy and kind. I've been fearful and ashamed. Thank you in advance for listening."

Does the thought of speaking the truth to your man about your secret scare you to death? Yes, I thought so. That's why you have kept it a secret so long. Don't rush into the living room right now and tell him everything you've avoided divulging since you've known him. Take some time to think, pray, and talk to a counselor or wise friend about it first. Then devise a plan for how you want to talk to him—if telling him is the wise thing to do. But by all means, tell somebody. Don't let your past poison your life any longer.

In the Word: Chapter Five Application

This chapter may have been difficult to read. We discussed the power and pain of hidden secrets—the ghosts in our closets. And now you may be wondering, *How in the world can I deal with my past and survive?* Or *Where do I begin to let go?*

There is hope! You can live in freedom today. First, you must understand what God's Word says about sin—personal sin and sin committed against you.

Secret Sin

> The Word of God is living and active, sharper than any two-edged sword, piercing to the division of soul and of spirit,

of joints and of marrow, and discerning the thoughts and intentions of the heart. And no creature is hidden from his sight, but all are naked and exposed to the eyes of him to whom we must give account (Hebrews 4:12-13 ESV).

The realization that we cannot hide from God can be scary. He sees our sin—we are naked and exposed. He sees our past and knows what is underneath the masks we so carefully use to hide our pain every day. A prayer of Moses recorded in Psalms says, "You have set our iniquities before you, our secret sins in the light of your presence" (Psalm 90:8 ESV). Compare Moses' prayer with these New Testament words: "This is the message we have heard from him and declare to you: God is light; in him there is no darkness at all. If we claim to have fellowship with him yet walk in the darkness, we lie and do not live by the truth" (1 John 1:5-6).

Have you ever experienced total, complete, and utter darkness? The darkness that exists when you turn off your helmet light in the belly of a cavern and you can't even see your hand in front of your face? When someone lights a candle or turns a helmet light back on, everyone is amazed at its power. What was once unseen is now seen—uncovered and clear. God is light in its most powerful form. He is pure, holy, and righteous.

We talked about three main areas that women across the country report as issues that continue to haunt them on a daily basis: abortion, sexual promiscuity, and walking away from people they love. Let's see what Scripture has to say about the way we handle each one.

Abortion

Emotional side effects from an abortion can be devastating. Depression, intense grief, anxiety, guilt, and shame are common postabortion symptoms. Psalm 139:16 (NKJV) says, "Your eyes saw my substance, being yet unformed. And in Your book they all were written, the days fashioned for me, when as yet there were none of them." The Bible clearly explains that life begins at conception and continues in the mother's womb and after the precious baby is born into this world. To purposely stop this process is against God's plan and is sin. However, I am so glad we serve a God who is faithful and just!

> If we walk in the light, as he is in the light, we have fellowship with one another, and the blood of Jesus his Son cleanses us from all sin. If we say we have no sin, we deceive ourselves, and the truth is not in us. If we confess our sins, he is faithful and just to forgive us our sins and to cleanse us from all unrighteousness (1 John 1:7-9 ESV).

In order to experience freedom from abortion in your past, you must repent and seek God's forgiveness.

Sexual Promiscuity

The story of David paints a vivid picture of sexual promiscuity and adulterous behavior. David, described as a man after God's heart (Acts 13:22), looked upon a beautiful woman named Bathsheba and lusted after her. Even though she was married, David had sex with her and then tried to cover his sin. The story goes on to say that David even sent her husband to the front lines of battle, knowing he would be killed, in order to take Bathsheba as his own wife (2 Samuel 11).

An adulterous and promiscuous past can be the source of tremendous guilt and deep pain. When sexual sin is kept hidden and is not confessed to God, a healthy marriage cannot exist. Later in Scripture we see that David realized his need to confess his sexual promiscuity and adultery: "I acknowledged my sin to you, and I did not cover my iniquity; I said, 'I will confess my transgressions to the LORD,' and you forgave the iniquity of my sin" (Psalm 32:5 ESV). David is praising God for His grace and forgiveness. That same grace and forgiveness is available to you.

Broken Relationships

We are created for relationships. When those relationships are severed, regardless of the reason, we are hurt. Women are especially vulnerable because we are created by God to be the more relational of the two sexes. Whether the broken relationship is a result of sin or miscommunication, reconciliation is always possible if both parties agree to try. If one party is not prepared to reconcile, the other party can at least become willing and gain a clear conscience.

First Peter 3:9 says, "Do not repay evil with evil or insult with insult, but with blessing, because to this you were called so that you may inherit a blessing." Jesus taught His disciples about restoring relationships:

> If your brother sins against you, go and show him his fault, just between the two of you. If he listens to you, you have won your brother over. But if he will not listen, take one or two others along, so that "every matter may be established by the testimony of two or three witnesses." If he refuses to listen to them, tell it to the church; and if he refuses to listen even to the church, treat him as you would a pagan or a tax collector (Matthew 18:15-17).

As we saw earlier in this chapter, the refusal to talk about past broken relationships can seriously erode our most cherished relationships today.

Forgiving Others

Forgiveness is about releasing the resentment that has kept you in emotional turmoil since the offense first took place. It also involves giving up the right for revenge. And it's never easy. Paul instructs the believers at the church of Ephesus to follow God's example: "Get rid of all bitterness, rage and anger, brawling and slander, along with every form of malice. Be kind and compassionate to one another, forgiving each other, just as in Christ God forgave you" (Ephesians 4:31-32). Letting go of the hurt and pain can bring tremendous freedom.

Keep in mind that forgiveness does not mean you are handing the person who has offended you a "get out of jail free" card. When you forgive, you are handing your offender to God to deal with as He sees fit.

Forgiving Ourselves

Forgiving ourselves can be harder than forgiving those who hurt us. When we have sinned and are dealing with intense guilt, shame, regret, and pain over that sin, we can hardly fathom that God chooses to forgive us. But He does!

Forgiveness is all about *choice*. In order to forgive yourself, you must *choose* to let go and forgive. God has already made His choice to forgive you, as we have seen in Ephesians 4. I could go on to explain steps to forgiveness and suggest many great books to read on the topic of forgiveness, but the bottom line is this: Forgiveness is a choice you must decide to make for yourself! No one can make the choice for you.

Reflection Questions

1. Do you struggle with the fear of being exposed if someone knew the truth about you? Have you been keeping secrets that seem too big to let go? Take a moment now to reflect on your past sins. Spend time in prayer, asking God to bring any unconfessed sin to mind so you can confess it and receive cleansing.

2. Do you have difficulty making the choice to forgive others? Is choosing to forgive yourself even harder?

3. How has your marriage or current dating relationship been

affected by choices you made in the past? Are these choices continuing to have an impact on your marriage or dating relationship today? Can you make any new choices now that will have a positive impact? Take the time to make an "I choose..." list. Make sure to write down the time and date on your list for future reference. Then commit this list to God and follow through.

I'm not telling him about...

6 How I Feel About Myself

Laugh a lot, and when you're older, all your wrinkles will be in the right places.

YOU MAY HAVE NATURAL BEAUTY. I don't. I never leave my house or have guests over without wearing makeup. Every Monday, Wednesday, and Friday morning I pick up my daughter, Megan, at her college dorm, and we go to our workout class together. It's mother-daughter time. But even then, I have my makeup on. I even wake up extra early most mornings that I take Zach to school to be sure I am ready before I start my day. Call it crazy or whatever you like, but I know this: When I have my makeup on, I feel a lot better about myself. Some people say, "If the barn needs a painting, then paint it." Most importantly, I know my appearance is important to Tim—just as it would be to any man who is breathing—and I want him to know I know that.

But this can become a problem for women like me when looking good consumes our thoughts, controls our lives, and defines who we are. How does that happen?

Some of us are old enough to remember the funny mirrors at county fairs. And if you're a younger girl reading this book, well, maybe you've seen them at Ripley's Believe It or Not or a fun house at Halloween. When we walk past one, we look like we're hippos—short and fat. Then we walk past another one that makes us look like we're ten feet tall and razor thin (I like that one!). One makes us look squiggly, and in another we have a huge body and a little head (I hate that one!). Regardless of the mirror we look into, we're fascinated by what we see.

The Mirrors We Look In

We look in mirrors every day—the mirrors of our husbands' expressions as they look at us. From the look in their eyes and the expressions on their faces, we get glimpses of ourselves. Sometimes we look gorgeous. Sometimes, not so gorgeous.

> One heart cannot reject or be rejected by another heart— a heart can only allow and be allowed room to grow.
>
> LAURA TERESA MARQUEZ

Psychologists (and everyone who observes people very closely at all) recognize that people's number one desire is to be accepted, and not surprisingly, our number one fear is to be rejected. Oscar-winning actress Celeste Holm stated, "We live by encouragement and die without it—slowly, sadly, angrily." Encouragement is the language of acceptance. All of us need it, and in fact, we can't really live without it. We long for the look in our husbands' eyes to tell us we're lovely, desirable, welcome, interesting, beautiful, and delicious. We don't have to see all this in their expressions all the time. They can portion these reflections out any way they like!

But our men aren't the only mirrors we look into. Actually, we've had a lifetime of looking into the mirrors of our parents, siblings, friends, mentors, and bosses. Anyone whose opinion we valued has been an important mirror in our lives. When we looked at these people, we noticed their response to us in their facial expressions, gestures, and words. We may think that words are the most important communication tool, but studies show that they comprise only 7 percent of a communicator's impact. Gestures and expressions account for all the rest. That's why our hearts aren't always moved when someone says, "I love you," but the look in his eyes say something else.

Many of us enter into relationships with men after we've been wounded by the mirrors we've looked into for years and we've learned to be suspicious of what we see. The reflections may be good and loving, but we don't trust our vision anymore. For that reason, we can't always blame our men if we don't believe the reflection we see.

The people around us are important mirrors in our lives, and the culture busily reflects its message all day, every day. Many studies show that women are portrayed in a sexual manner far more often than men (by being dressed in revealing clothing, with body postures or facial expressions that imply sexual readiness) and are objectified (they are used as a decorative object, or they display specific body parts instead of the whole person). In addition, physical beauty is prized over any other attribute. These models of femininity are presented for young girls to study and emulate.[1]

When we look at gorgeous women in ads in magazines, on the red carpet at the Academy Awards, in movies, and on television, we're looking into our culture's standard of what's acceptable, and the vast majority of us can't measure up! One study states that women view an average of about 500 advertisements each day, creating distorted expectations and misperceptions about their bodies. Advertisers often sell their products by emphasizing sexuality and physical attractiveness. The effect is that

> Beauty—in projection and perceiving—is 99.9 percent attitude.
> GREY LIVINGSTON

many women are preoccupied with their body image, and this often results in unhealthy behavior as women strive for ultrathin bodies idealized by the media. A recent poll by *People* magazine found that "80 percent of women reported that the images of women in advertisements make them feel insecure about their looks." In addition, the poll indicated that 34 percent of women are willing to try diets that pose health risks, 34 percent are willing to go "under the knife," and 93 percent said they had made various and repeated attempts to lose weight to measure up to the advertised images. Why do the media spend so much time and effort making us feel bad about ourselves? It's all about the dollars. Women who have bought into these images spend billions on cosmetics, new diets, and clothes.

> Taking joy in living is a woman's best cosmetic.
> ROSALIND RUSSELL

The purpose of advertising is to create discontent. In his book *The Technological Society,* French cultural analyst Jacques Ellul makes this observation:

> One of the great designs of advertising is to create needs; but this is possible only if these needs correspond to an ideal of life that man accepts. The way of life offered by advertising is all the more compelling in that it corresponds to certain easy and simple tendencies of man and refers to a world in which there are no spiritual values to form and inform life. When men feel and respond to the needs advertising creates, they are adhering to its ideal of life. The human tendencies upon which advertising like this is based may be strikingly simpleminded, but they nonetheless represent pretty much the level of our modern life. Advertising offers us the ideal we have always wanted (and that ideal is certainly not a heroic way of life).[2]

Ellul's insights are brilliant and piercing. The "ideal" life depicted in modern advertising promises to fulfill our expectations of wealth, ease, happiness, and—for women—startling beauty. Reflexively, we compare our shape, our skin, our eyes, our hair, the shape of our feet, our nails, and every other physical feature to the most beautiful women on the planet. No wonder many of us feel so bad about ourselves! Why do we focus so much on being beautiful? Dale Carnegie stated succinctly, "We are creatures of emotion, bristling with prejudice and motivated by pride and vanity."

> Beauty isn't worth thinking about; what's important is your mind. You don't want a fifty-dollar haircut on a fifty-cent head.
>
> GARRISON KEILLOR

Pop Quiz

So then, do you think the mirrors you look in—your man's expressions and the media's pictures of beautiful women—don't have any impact on how you feel about yourself? That's possible, but it's not very likely. We are inundated by these messages, and we long to be validated. Our thirst for approval is built into our DNA. We look for it wherever we think we can find it, but we dread the prospect of uncovering the look of rejection that says, "Sorry, honey, but you just don't measure up."

Let me give you a pop quiz. Here are a few easy questions to answer:

- How much time do you spend in front of a mirror every day?
- How often do you look into mirrors when you're not dressing?
- In one or two words, how do you feel as you're looking into the mirror?

- On average per day, how much time do you look at images of gorgeous women in magazines, on television, and in movies?

- In one or two words, how do you feel about yourself as you look at those images?

- What did you see when you looked in the mirror of your parents?

- What do you see most often when you look in the mirror of your man's eyes?

Okay, that's enough for now. How did you do on the quiz? If you're like most of us, you don't even think about those issues because they are so much a part of everyday life. But here's another question: When you're upset, what names do you call yourself? The answer to that question is a good indication of who you really believe you are. I posed that question to a close friend of mine, and she thought long and hard before she gave me an answer. Finally, her eyes glistened and her voice quaked as she told me, "Julie, I'm embarrassed to tell you the words I use. They're not fit to speak out loud."

I asked gently, "What do you think those names say about you?"

She replied instantly with the wide eyes of insight, "If I heard someone say those things about another person, I'd have to conclude that she *hated* that person. Hate. Yes, that's what it really is."

The Roles People Play

To a significant extent, the shape of the mirrors we gaze into each day is as accurate or as distorted as the health of our family of origin. The more dysfunctional our families, the more we felt compelled to play roles. These roles are designed to accomplish three objectives:

1. to protect us from experiencing more pain,

2. to provide us with some sense of meaning in a crazy world, and

3. to help us control something—anything!—so we feel
   safer.

Some of us came from relatively healthy families where trust, love, and honesty were treasured, but some of us felt terribly unsafe when we were children. To try to make sense of life, we found roles to play. Here are some common ones.

The hero. This person is driven to excel in some area like academics or athletics to prove he's valuable and worthy of esteem. Receiving accolades also deflects attention off of the shame of the family and onto the one who is praiseworthy.

The princess. Like the hero, this girl excels, but she is praised for her beauty and poise. Being the center of attention feels good, but it never completely satisfies because she's always measuring herself by other girls' beauty. She is always at risk of falling short.

The mascot or clown. When family tensions rise, this person makes jokes, speaks one-liners, and tells stories to divert attention from the problem, ease the pressure, and lower the friction level. To cover her own pain, she laughs when she's hurt, angry, or nervous.

The enabler. In needy families, this person gets her identity from fixing everybody's problems. She plays the role of a savior, jumping in to rescue people from their own problems instead of letting them suffer (and learn from) the consequences of their bad choices. If she sees a need, she meets it. If she sees a small need, she says it's catastrophic so she can feel good about herself when she meets it. If she can't find a problem to fix, she'll stir one up so she can fix it.

The scapegoat. In families where anger continues to escalate and people don't offer forgiveness, somebody has to take the blame. Quite often, one person is singled out as the sponge to soak up all the blame for everyone else's sins and mistakes. One woman told me that she was blamed for her father's drug addiction, her sister's pregnancy, and her brother running away from home. "If it hadn't been for you," her mother screamed at her, "none of this would have happened!"

The lost child. In these emotionally abusive families, some children want to distance themselves from the tension as much as possible. They've given up on finding resolution. Their goal is to get as far away as they can and to hide—in their rooms, behind a book, or in a television show. A friend told me that when she was a child, her violent parents sometimes commented, "Jimmy gave us plenty to worry about, but Jennifer never gave us any trouble at all." Yes, when you're invisible, you don't cause any problems.

The volcano. What happens to angry people? A few of them become volcanoes. They may smolder for weeks or even months, but sooner or later, they blow like Mount St. Helens! They use their rage to intimidate others in the family, and after just a few of these outbursts, everyone fears the next explosion. People walk on eggshells around these people because they're so afraid of setting off a blast of rage.

When I've explained these roles, people have asked several questions. For example, where do addicts and abusers fit into these roles? Quite often, they played one of these roles as a child, but the pain proved so great that they felt they had to medicate it with drugs, alcohol, food, sex, or gambling. And people who experienced abuse often become abusive themselves. The only models they saw as children were those who hurt others to control them, and though they felt terrible pain from these experiences, it's the only game they know to play.

People have also asked if their roles can change. Yes, they can. A cataclysmic event can shake up the whole family and shift the roles they play. A friend told me that when she was ten years old, everybody's role changed in her family because of her father's heart attack. Her mother had been an enabler for her father's addiction, but now she became a volcano. Her brother had been a hero, but he became the scapegoat. She had been a mascot, but now she took the hero role.

Do you see how each member of the family is a mirror that distorts everyone else's image? Day after day and year after year, children in these families look into the faces of their parents and siblings, and the reflection tells them they aren't safe, they have to play roles to find some sense of meaning, and they have to control all the crazy people to limit the pain. These mirrors are terribly distorted.

Seeing Yourself through a Different Mirror

Change, and especially change in our perceptions, doesn't happen without a flash of insight like the one my friend had. For her, this moment became a turning point. For years, she had lived in a secret world of self-doubt and self-blame, a destructive perspective fueled by a host of negative mirrors from her past. Her husband was one of her most accurate and positive mirrors, but she struggled to embrace his love and acceptance because she felt she wasn't worthy. On this day, though, things began to change. A shaft of light penetrated into the darkness of her secret world, and she saw she had choices about what she thought about herself. She began choosing to recite names for herself from God's Word: *loved, forgiven, adopted, chosen*...and she didn't have to go farther than Ephesians 1 to find all those and more.

For years, she had studied the Bible, but a barrier had always stood between her secrets and God's powerful truth. But no longer. As she read the Gospels in a new light, she realized that Jesus delighted in showering His love on real people—prostitutes, tax gatherers, lepers, and other outcasts. She was one of them! She read about people who erected barriers to keep Christ out. He offered His love, but they refused to accept it. She didn't want any barriers to block the flow of God's love any longer.

For the first time in her life, she began to feel loved and beautiful in God's eyes. It was thrilling and liberating! In a few weeks, the look on her face was transformed more than any amount of makeup could do. Her smile was genuine, no longer forced. Her eyes sparkled instead of appearing dull and lifeless. Everything about her began to radiate a new joy and confidence. How did it happen? She became honest with God about her self-perception, and her honesty was an open door for Him to walk in and flood her life with His grace. Oh, she still struggles with fleeting feelings of not measuring up, of being unworthy and unacceptable, but she knows how to fight against them now. They no longer consume and oppress her. Today, they are just part of life's battle to walk with God, enjoy His presence, and bask in His love.

Outer Beauty—Does It Matter?

A few months ago I met with a woman who asked me for help. Her children were out of control, and her marriage was falling apart. In fact, her husband had another interest, and she knew her. "Julie," she said, "I could never live up to that woman. I think I've lost my husband."

> **Beauty**, n: the power by which a woman charms a lover and terrifies a husband.
>
> AMBROSE BIERCE

As I looked her in the eyes, tears flowing from both of us, I asked her, "What do you mean, you can't live up to her?"

"Well, she's beautiful. And you know what? I don't even wear makeup anymore. I've stopped watching what I eat, and I gave up exercising too. I figured he wasn't into me, so why should I bother?"

I was stunned. Here was a woman I knew years ago as one of the most beautiful and fit women I knew. And here she sat, dejected, noticeably heavier than years ago, and exhausted. Let me use this opportunity to tell you that our beauty is cyclical. I know and appreciate those who say that inner beauty is all that matters. But let me tell you something…I have yet to meet a woman who knows her worth, is confident and beautiful on the inside, and who didn't take care of herself on the outside.

When we're feeling rejected or depressed, we usually let our outward appearance become a direct reflection of what's going on inside. And one way to stop that from happening is to feel good about ourselves on the outside. Self-care is to a woman what a salary is to a man.

Sure, beauty is only skin deep, but feeling confident about your outward appearance reflects and influences your inner beliefs.

What Your Man Needs

At the county fair or the fun house, the mirrors are fixed and inanimate. They don't care how people look back at them. The men in our lives, though, are not only mirrors for us—they care deeply about the kind of mirrors we are for them. Countless women have said, "All I've ever wanted is for someone to love me." But most professional counselors report they have rarely met a *man* who doesn't feel exactly the same way. Men are just not as obvious or verbal about their need for love.

> Since love grows within you, so beauty grows. For love is the beauty of the soul.
> SAINT AUGUSTINE

When a man looks into the face of his wife or girlfriend, he longs for the same unconditional acceptance we want, and he dreads seeing the rejection we also fear. Most men simply aren't very articulate about their feelings or perceptive about their hopes and fears. These things just don't seem manly. In their world, chainsaws, paychecks, and ball games measure their worth. We could certainly argue that a woman's world is just as competitive as any man's, but for now, let's at least acknowledge that he feels tremendous pressure to succeed. The dynamic is much more complicated than this, but we could say that we compare beauty, but men compare promotions. We are, whether we realize it or not, in the same boat of living for a word of encouragement and dying without it. In fact, some authorities believe that men are even more desperate for love because they feel so isolated and lonely.

To explain how they show their love for us, most men would say something like this: "I work hard, bring home a paycheck, try to take good care of the kids, and I try to pick up around the house a little."

When we understand that their love for us is just as strong as our love for them—but that they show it differently—the look in our eyes changes from demands to gratitude. Do you think they notice? You bet they do. When our men realize that we genuinely appreciate how much they do for us, they relax, the tension between us subsides, and we are both able to give and receive a little more love.

What You Can Say to Him

Before we say anything to our husbands about all of this, we need to get a handle on the mirrors in our lives. We need to understand how the expressions of our parents, our bosses, and others have shaped our self-perception, and we need to grasp how strong our culture's impact has been on the shape of our inner lives. Most of us should take a few steps toward healing and change before we share much with our men. Then we can say something like this: "Let me tell you some things I've been learning." We can share perceptions about mirrors from our past and the impact of advertising. We can explain that some mirrors have been good and healthy but some have been harmful. And we can tell them about the steps of progress we've made.

When you think about the names you've called yourself, remember that your man has probably called himself names just as awful when he's upset. Maybe you've heard them and maybe you haven't, but I've never known a man who didn't have some choice names reserved for himself when he's messed up. When you feel comfortable telling him about your negative self-talk, you may provide a platform for him to say, "Yeah? Well, I do the same thing." And another link has formed to strengthen your relationship.

If your inner fears of rejection have prompted you to act in self-destructive ways, begin a healing process by admitting your situation to yourself and to God and then to someone you trust—perhaps the man in your life. Fears are incredibly powerful, and they dramatically affect our sense of acceptance and beauty. They drive us to shop, drink, gossip, starve ourselves, and binge to find comfort. I have seen it all too often in the lives of the women I mentor.

In our conversations with our men, we need to avoid any hint of demanding a specific response. We may want them to touch us and hug us to communicate just the right message to us, but if we demand these things, we create more barriers. We can speak the truth and share what's on our hearts, but then we need to let them choose how to respond. Many men respond to honesty quickly, but some feel uncomfortable when we talk openly and honestly about our feelings. Know your man, and share as much and as quickly as is appropriate. You may have taken weeks or months to think about the mirrors in your life. Give him at least ten minutes!

Certainly, one of the things to say to him is thank you. Be a good mirror and reflect back to him your gratitude for all he does for you and the family. Point out specific things you appreciate, and encourage him about those. I've learned that praise and encouragement are effective only when they are targeted. If we say, "You're great!" people are likely to wonder what we mean, decide that we don't know them very well, or doubt our sincerity. We communicate more powerfully when we say, "You did this well and that well, and I saw how that person responded when you did so and so. I appreciate your thoughtfulness and willingness to help."

The husband of a good friend told me that his wife is the most thankful woman in the world. Wow, that's quite a statement from a man! I know this couple, and he certainly has his share of quirks and faults, but somewhere in their relationship, she chose to be as positive a mirror as she could possibly be. Oh, she's honest with him about his mess ups when she feels she needs to be, but the pattern of her communication is overwhelmingly positive. He knows in his bones that she really loves him, and he reflects that same unconditional love back to her. It's a beautiful thing to see. I don't know where their relationship would be if she had focused on his faults instead of his strengths, but I can tell you this for sure: It would be a completely different relationship.

I have one more recommendation for you. One of the most important decisions we can make is to filter the messages that come into our minds and saturate our hearts. Some of us need to do radical surgery to cut out most, if not all, of our time gazing at beautiful women in ads. Jesus said we should be in the world but not of the world. For me, that means that I spend enough time to know what's going on in the culture, but I have to guard my heart to be sure the culture's values don't consume me.

Look at fewer magazines, and skip the ads in them and read only the articles. Instead of dwelling on how much you want to look like this model or that one, take the time to plan how you'll show appreciation to your husband or memorize an encouraging passage of Scripture. We can't totally escape all the distorted mirrors, but we can avoid staring at them and ignore some altogether.

The way we feel about ourselves is a product of the messages we've seen in the mirrors of our lives. The good news is that we don't have to keep believing them. With some insight from a friend, the truth of God's Word, the strength of the Holy Spirit, and a dab of courage, we can take steps toward love and acceptance. Along the way, we can tell our men what's going on in our hearts. And who knows—maybe God will use us to touch them more deeply than ever before.

In the Word: Chapter Six Application

Oh, the feelings we women battle with! Most important among them is our longing to be beautiful—especially in our husbands' eyes. Just as the queen asked the mirror in the Grimm brothers' tale, we ask our men in a thousand ways, "Mirror, mirror, on the wall, who in this land is fairest of all?"

With all our hearts, we hope beyond all hope that our men will reply quite differently than the magic mirror did in the story. Maybe something more like this: "Some women are fair; it is true. But you, my dear, are a thousand times more beautiful than any other."

Why do we so deeply long to be beautiful? Why are we so hurt when we don't feel beautiful? Because God, the essence of beauty, created us in His image. My dictionary defines *beauty* as "excellence," and in Psalms, David bursts out, "O LORD, our Lord, how excellent is Your name in all the earth!" (Psalm 8:1 NKJV). Let's dive into God's Word and try to make sense of how we feel about ourselves.

Why Beauty?

Beauty comes from God. As much as we try to curl and tuck and enhance, true beauty is deeper than that. It has to do with something deep within our souls. Our feminine longing to be beautiful is ultimately connected to our longing for God Himself. God's beauty was so attractive to King David that he claimed it was the only thing worth pursuing! "One thing I ask of the LORD, this is what I seek: that I may dwell in the house of the LORD all the days of my life, to gaze upon the beauty of the LORD and to seek him in his temple" (Psalm 27:4).

When one of your girlfriends shows up to a party with a cute jacket or a stunning dress, what is the first thing out of your mouth? I usually ask, "Where'd you get it?" Beauty is an expression of the designer and points back to him or her. Solomon saw that the same is true with God: "He has made everything beautiful in its time" (Ecclesiastes 3:11). If God is the author of beauty, then it makes sense that His creation would be beautiful. No kidding! Just look around you at the mountains, the flowers, the sunsets...and you.

Everything. That includes you. Do you really get that? No, really. "The king is enthralled by your beauty; honor him, for he is your lord" (Psalm 45:11). God doesn't make ugly things or ugly people. He can't. It goes against His very nature. God's Word says you are beautiful!

Are you short? You are beautiful. Are you tall? You are beautiful. Do you have a model body? You are beautiful. Are you rather ordinary? You are beautiful. Let that truth sink deep into your heart.

The Heart of It All

Our world defines beauty in terms of figure and form, but God says quite the opposite! "The LORD does not look at the things man looks at. Man looks at the outward appearance, but the LORD looks at the heart" (1 Samuel 16:7). According to God's Word, your girlfriend who is fighting breast cancer is just as beautiful as Hollywood's hottest celebrity—maybe *more* beautiful! God wants you to rejoice in your unique beauty, and that goes far deeper than your skin.

We all have bad hair days. But how often do we neglect the thoughts and intentions of our hearts while trying to find our security in how we look? It won't work. This is the very problem Jesus saw in the religious leaders of his day: "You are like whitewashed tombs, which look beautiful on the outside but on the inside are full of dead men's bones and everything unclean" (Matthew 23:27).

God is talking about your heart—the deepest part of who you are. Too often, we rely only on our "stuff" to make us beautiful, and we forget the most important part, which no one but God sees. In the Old Testament, God judges His people for this very reason:

> You trusted in your beauty and used your fame to become a prostitute. You lavished your favors on anyone who passed by and your beauty became his. You took some of your garments to make gaudy high places, where you carried on your prostitution. Such things should not happen, nor should they ever occur. You also took the fine jewelry I gave you, the jewelry made of my gold and silver, and you made for yourself male idols and engaged in prostitution with them (Ezekiel 16:15-19).

At times, I catch myself "downing" my makeup job, the dress that doesn't feel quite right, the way my hair looks...and on it goes. The devil knows that beauty is powerful. And he, the expert deceiver, will use our little imperfections to whisper little lies into our minds:

> You're ugly.
>
> You're no good.
>
> No one could ever love you.
>
> You have nothing to offer.
>
> You aren't worth it...

...and the list goes on! Do you notice a common word here? *You.* Satan will try to get you to focus on yourself and on the ways you couldn't possibly be nearly as good or beautiful or smart or talented as the women around you.

Paul warns the Corinthians against this very thing: "But when they measure themselves by one another, and compare themselves with one another, they are without understanding" (2 Corinthians 10:12 RSV). In sorting through how you feel about yourself, stop and think about whom you have been comparing yourself to. How have those comparisons made you feel?

Breaking the Mirrors

All of us have been shaped by the "mirrors" in our lives...our parents, our teachers, our boyfriends, our husbands. And sometimes that influence can mess up the way we see ourselves. But we all know that physical beauty doesn't last forever. "Charm is deceptive, and beauty is fleeting; but a woman who fears the LORD is to be praised" (Proverbs 31:30).

Wrinkles happen. But God's view of you is not based on something so shallow. Every time Satan tries to attack you with lies about you being ugly or not good enough, try fighting back with this: Jesus did not die for nothing. He died for you. Even when you were dead in your sin, He saw you as precious—so precious that He spilled His blood for you!

When we beat ourselves down and live in a negative mind-set, we are failing to fully accept the sacrifice of Jesus! Sure, sometimes we look in the mirror and just want to crawl back in bed. But your *feelings* about how beautiful or talented or loveable you may or may not be are not accurate indicators of who you really are. The real you goes much deeper than that.

The devil often tries to trip us up with our feelings. We women feel things very deeply, and other people's snide remarks often play like an irritating jingle we can't forget, reinforcing our negative feelings about ourselves. But if Satan can keep you focused on how you feel (which gives you a distorted understanding of yourself), you'll quickly forget what God says about you (which is the truth).

Regardless of the mirrors of condemnation you've looked in, regardless of what other people have told you, this is what God has to say about you:

> The LORD your God is in your midst,
>   a mighty one who will save;
>   he will rejoice over you with gladness;
>   he will quiet you by his love;
>   he will exult over you with loud singing
>   (Zephariah 3:17 ESV).

Loud singing. God is crazy about you! And not because of anything you've done or any new hairdo…He's crazy about you because He created you—beautifully! For too long, we've defined our worth by looking into mirrors that are clouded by sin. Those mirrors reflect Satan's lies that lead to self-condemnation and self-hatred. Will you break those mirrors today?

God's Word talks about the importance of "your inner self, the unfading beauty of a gentle and quiet spirit, which is of great worth in God's sight" (1 Peter 3:4). *That* is real beauty. God wants you to live in the truth of who He says you are. And in the end, His opinion is the most important!

Talking to Your Man

You may be thinking, *Great, Julie—I got that. But how do I talk to my husband about it?* Once you've gotten a handle on who you really are according to the truth of God, the next good and healthy step is to share with your husband what you've been feeling. If you've struggled with negative self-talk, he probably has too. Being honest with him about the way you see yourself and what God is teaching you is an effective way to create intimacy.

A lot of times we women expect our men to know exactly how we feel. But stop and think about it: How is he going to know unless you tell him? Opening up about what's really going on with you can be uncomfortable. No joke! But resorting to the age-old "I'm fine" is actually lying. God's Word says, "Therefore each of you must put off falsehood and speak truthfully to his neighbor, for we are all members of one body" (Ephesians 4:25). If you are not honest with him, how can you expect him to be honest with you?

First, start by being honest with God about how you're feeling. God's doesn't want religious tirades or canned spiritual prayers. He wants *you* to talk to Him. If you can't be honest with the God who loves you unconditionally, how can you open up your heart to the man you love?

Then talk with your man. Let him help you journey through your negative self-talk. He may need to provide the positive affirmations you need in order to overcome the negative self-talk you don't need.

Reflection Questions

1. In this chapter, we talked about the mirrors we look into—the people who influence us. What mirrors are you looking into? What mirrors have wounded you most? How have you been hurt by those people's words?

2. How do you feel about *you?* What negative self-talk are you repeating? On a blank piece of paper, make two columns. On one side, write each of the negative comments you make to yourself most often. In the other column, beside each negative statement, write a verse that replaces the negative lie with the truth of God's Word. Memorize each verse. Repeat each one throughout the day.

3. Knowing God's truth and affirming it at the core of your being is the only way to get free. How can you begin today to begin to build a healthy view of yourself? How can you involve your man in that process?

I'm not telling him about...

7 How He Hurts Me

The only time a woman really succeeds in changing a man is when he's a baby.

SHERYL CROW DID A REMAKE OF THE OLD SONG *The First Cut Is the Deepest*. You're probably singing it even now. When a girl gets married, she expects life to be special, and she expects her man to be "someone to be there for me, to hold me, to never hurt me"…at least not intentionally. But every relationship goes through times when it is not the way it is supposed to be, and in every relationship, people get hurt occasionally. The first cut goes deep. Problems increase when that wound is reopened again and again, and the hurt sometimes turns to harm.

I hope your relationship is based on trust and respect, but in my years of talking to women around the country, I've found too many who experience deep and daily hurts from the men they hoped would cherish them. Sometimes these hurts are subtle and even unintentional. Others, though, are intentional. Some women are trapped in relationships they have no clue how to get out of. Their men are withholding love, putting them down, calling them names, controlling them, and more. These men may even be forcing sexual activity, grabbing, choking, slapping, punching, or threatening to hurt their wives or children.

Big Girls Don't Cry

We're often told that hurt is just a part of relationships, as if we should keep a stiff upper lip and not even bring it up because that would possibly make things worse. We're told big girls don't cry. Too often when people think and act this way, hurt turns to harm.

For example, if he grew up in a home where yelling was the norm and she didn't, she won't get hysterical—she'll get historical and remember the time somebody yelled at her. Instead of telling him how his yelling has hurt her, she'll just stuff her feelings and not say anything so he won't yell again.

It all brings fire to my bones. There is *no* place for any of this behavior in relationships—period. But it happens. If the message of this chapter isn't for you personally, you probably know a friend or two who feels violated or even lives in a daily hell. "Approximately 33 million people (15 percent of all American adults) admit that they were victims of domestic violence. Furthermore, six in ten adults claim that they know someone personally who has experienced domestic violence."[1]

Sleeping with the Enemy

When wounded women first met their men, they admired their strength. They may have seen an outburst or two of frustration, but they thought, *No, he'd never treat me that way.* But he did, and he still does. Too many women wake up one day "sleeping with the enemy." Many of them, though, aren't objective about the pain they endure.

Over and over again, women find the courage to begin a conversation with me about their relationships but quickly backtrack and assume all the blame. "I'm sure I did something to set him off," they try to explain. "It's my fault. If I were a better lover, none of this would be happening." And the door of honesty quickly closes. Honesty, though, is a crucial step in finding resolution and healing.

Deep Wounds, Many Excuses

Most of the wounded women I've known aren't classic victims of the physical abuse we now call "inter-partner violence." When we talk, I often ask, "Has he hit you?"

> An injury is much sooner forgotten than an insult.
> LORD CHESTERFIELD

Quite often, they shake their heads and say something like, "No, he hasn't exactly hit me."

That wasn't exactly the clearest answer, so I follow up by asking, "What do you mean 'not exactly'?"

Some don't want to take the next step to be more vulnerable, so they change the subject, but others tell me about particular situations: "We got into an argument. He was yelling at me, accusing me of some things I didn't do. And then he grabbed me."

In these conversations, the level of fear these dear women experience goes through the roof, so I have to patiently and persistently continue to ask questions. "How did he grab you? Exactly what happened?"

In their description of physical abuse, women often minimize the damage, blame themselves, and excuse their men. As a result, an abusive cycle develops. In some cases, the physical wound is deep and lasting. By the most conservative estimate, a million American women experience domestic violence each year, but other authorities put the figure at four million.[2] But far more often, the wounds inflicted on women are not physically visible. But they are devastating, inflicting invisible emotional and psychological damage. To put handles on this problem—for you or for a friend—let's take a brief look at the types of wounds.

Abuse

Women may experience physical, sexual, or emotional abuse. Physical violence may take the form of hitting, slapping, punching, choking, cutting, shooting, grabbing, holding down, or pinching. Sexual abuse is any kind of inappropriate sexual contact, including a wide range of behaviors from forced intercourse to fondling to suggestive language. All kinds of overt abuse create emotional trauma, but the most common cause of damage occurs from verbal assaults: blaming, accusing, withdrawing, silence, and screaming, often accompanied by coldhearted stares.

Isolation

A particularly painful form of abuse occurs when people isolate themselves from us physically or emotionally. Some men walk out the door in a blind rage and don't come back for days, weeks, or even months. Some, though, stay in the house but refuse to talk. Both kinds of isolation are designed to punish us and control us—and they are amazingly and diabolically effective.

Choosing Someone or Something Else

One of the most tragic moments in a woman's life occurs when she realizes that her husband has chosen someone else instead of her. Most women in this situation suspect it for a long time but refuse to pursue it—precisely because it might be true! At the moment of exposure, the dream of being the only one in his life is shattered. Studies show that 3 to 4 percent of married people have sexual partners besides their spouses in a given year, and 15 to 18 percent of married people have had another sexual partner at some time while they've been married. Sadly, the statistics for Christian couples isn't significantly different.[3]

Emotional affairs are just as devastating but not as widely understood. I talked to a woman who confided that for months, she suspected that her husband was in contact with his high school sweetheart. For a long time, she tried to brush off her suspicions, but one day, she glanced at his PDA and saw an e-mail from her. It included content that was definitely inappropriate to send to a married man! She confronted him, and she found out the two had been corresponding by e-mail and phone for two years. They hadn't had sex, but the nature of the e-mail message indicated that the move from an emotional affair to sex wasn't far off.

I've talked with countless women who, with tears in their eyes, recount the story that their husbands or boyfriends love alcohol, drugs, pornography, or gambling more than them. These women have begged, pleaded, and threatened to try to get their men to change, but nothing has worked. Oh, a few times their men have said, "I'm sorry. I'll never do it again." But days later they were back to their old tricks.

Mixed Messages

When I've talked to women about the deep wounds they've experienced and the piercing disappointment they feel because their dreams of true love have been crushed, some of them look confused and tell me, "But Julie, he isn't like that all the time. Most of the time he's just fine, and sometimes he's wonderful."

I take that opportunity to explain the manipulative power of mixed messages. If he were always good and kind, we wouldn't be having the conversation, and if he were universally harmful, she would probably have the courage and clarity of mind to leave. But most abusive men intuitively know that mixed messages keep their women hooked. The blend of affirmation and accusation produces a combination of hope and fear in us—hope that he'll be sweet to us because we thirst for his tenderness and affection, but fear that he'll hurt us again. In response, we cling even tighter to him, excusing his harmful behavior because we long to be loved. Hope and fear form powerful handcuffs to keep us controlled. We need to set a no-excuse rule.

The Public Veneer

I've talked with women who told me, "I've wanted to talk to people in our church about him, but they wouldn't believe me. To them, he looks like the model husband and father: attentive, loving, and kind. But behind closed doors, he's a tyrant!" Some of these women have tried to reach out for help, but too often, they are seen as exaggerating the problem, so they get flippant advice and are sent back into the cauldron of pain.

Why We Stay Stuck

Women who find themselves in hurtful relationships don't just wake up one day and realize they're in trouble. Many of them grew up in families where trust had been shattered by addictions, abuse, or abandonment. They married men like their dads, and the results were all too predictable. Women in difficult relationships stay stuck for a variety of reasons. As you read these, remember the definition of insanity: doing the same thing but expecting different results.

Clueless in Seattle

Some of us have lived in painful, abusive relationships all our lives, and we don't have any concept that life could be any different. Every day, we're devoted to survival, not love and understanding. We're doing the best we can, but without objectivity, we're destined to "rearrange the deck chairs on the Titanic" instead of pursuing real change and healthy resolutions for relational problems. When we have brief flashes that "this just isn't working," we may take a halting step or two toward sanity, but we quickly get blasted (or isolated) back into our old role of quiet submission.

All My Fault

Deeply wounded people almost always have a distorted sense of responsibility. They blame themselves for their own problems, other people's behaviors and problems, and maybe even the national deficit. Accepting all the blame is their way of lowering the tension level. They know that if they spoke the truth to the abusers, they'd reap a whirlwind of expressions of anger, and they sure don't want to go through that again! Sooner or later, though, their "blame tank" gets full and overflows. At that point, they eagerly blame someone else for their faults and mistakes.

The Deep Well of Hurt and Anger

I talked to a lady who has lived for fifteen years with an angry, controlling husband. She told me, "For years, we argued loud and long, but after a while I couldn't take it anymore. I gave up, and for the past ten years, we haven't argued as much. Is that the right thing to do?"

I asked simply, "So, how is that working for you? What are you doing with all the anger?"

She instantly replied, "Oh, I have a lot of resentment toward him."

No kidding. Unresolved hurt and anger (they're flip sides of the same coin) poison every aspect of our lives. We may think we have good reasons to close the door on abusive men because we don't see any way to relieve the pain and heal the hurts, but as our sores fester, they cloud our thinking, rob us of joy, and distort every relationship in our lives. Instead of gladly giving to others and serving them, we need them to fix our hurts, so we demand that they treat us a certain way. Of course, they don't know that we're expecting them to heal gaping wounds in our hearts, so they soon disappoint us. Because they let us down, we add them to the list of people we're mad at, and we move on to someone else. Let me say it again—your past isn't your past if it's affecting your present.

Fragile

Women who live under a crushing mountain of abuse and fear become very fragile, and that makes them even more vulnerable. It's like having a broken arm—if anyone gives it even the slightest bump, it hurts like crazy! And we get bumped all day every day by our men, by our kids, at work, with our friends...in every situation in our lives.

Living this way takes a toll on our confidence. If we ever felt good about ourselves, we don't any longer. Shame is the perception that we're unworthy of anybody's love. We're hopeless, helpless victims, and we'll always be that way.

Dancing Around the Problem

One of the saddest parts of the stories abused women tell is that they have no hope for change. Instead of facing the reality of their situations, they felt they could only try to manage their men's rage, minimize the damage by complying with every demand, and find some sense of peace and joy in the children or somewhere else. They live in silence under the threat of revenge if they speak out. When women have the courage to talk to me, I sometimes ask, "How long have you lived this way?"

They often tell me it's been going on for years. Years! Every day is horrible, but they didn't see any way out. I then ask, "Why didn't you tell anybody before now?"

Almost invariably, their eyes open wide and they say, "Julie, you have no idea how angry he would be if he knew I'm talking to you now."

The choice to deal with an abusive relationship isn't like choosing what to have for dinner tonight. No, it's pretty close to life and death. Speaking the truth is terribly threatening. It risks instigating more rage, condemnation, and violence than ever before.

We aren't conditioned to live under this kind of stress for very long. Sooner or later, we break down emotionally and physically. Some women in abusive relationships turn to food, kids, pills, illegal drugs, or alcohol to mask their pain and give them some relief. Many more live in the deafening silence of depression, feeling completely hopeless, without energy or purpose to go on. And many others suffer under the constant strain of anxiety. Surveys report that almost 20 percent of adults in America experience anxiety disorders each year.[4]

Clearing Away Some Confusion

Women in abusive relationships desperately need someone to come alongside them. If that's you, find a professional Christian counselor or a pastor skilled in helping victims of abuse. If the abuse is violent, consider going immediately to a women's shelter. And if you know someone in this situation, don't give simplistic answers like "Just pray about it" or "Trust God and it will go away." Be a shoulder to cry on, a listening ear, and a source of strength during your friend's climb out of the darkness into light. Abused women need to begin to safely set healthy boundaries to limit the damage and find a sense of peace. In many cases, they feel tremendously guilty for even mentioning the problem. When they start taking action, they almost invariably feel terrified of the consequences.

Many Christian women feel confused about setting boundaries because they are encouraged to be obedient and submissive, even to abusive people. Various passages of Scripture are used to back up this fallacy, and confused women often feel obligated to go along—but they are furious at feeling controlled. We need a broader perspective on this issue, one that takes the full teaching of Scripture into account. God hates violence and would never expect you to live in an abusive relationship (Malachi 2:16). Let's look at three important principles.

The Right of Self-Protection

Some Bible teachers say that a Christian has no rights at all. In one sense, that is true. If we call Christ "Lord," we submit ourselves to His leading wherever He may direct us. But even though we may have no right to go against the will of God, He has given us the right and the responsibility to act appropriately in human relationships. As His beloved children, we are to be strong and wise. Jesus admonished us to be "wise as serpents and harmless as doves" (Matthew 10:16 NKJV). That means we are to understand the dynamics of motives and actions in relationships and to act with astute wisdom, not in manipulation or revenge.

When people abuse or control us, we are to protect ourselves. Paul warned Timothy about a man who had attacked him: "Alexander the metalworker did me a great deal of harm. The Lord will repay him for what he has done. You too should be on your guard against him, because he strongly opposed our message" (2 Timothy 4:14-15). In the same way, we need to be on guard against those who have hurt us or who threaten to hurt us. Being on guard, however, doesn't mean we counterattack. Paul's encouragement to Timothy was the assurance that God Himself would repay Alexander for hurting him. Protecting ourselves is entirely appropriate; taking revenge is not.

The Nature of Love

We are to submit first and foremost to the Lord, not to people. We are to obey Him at all costs and at all times. The question, then, is this: What is the Lord's will when we find ourselves in difficult situations? We find many passages in the Bible that instruct us to love one another, but many of us are confused about what it means to love an addict or an abusive person. If an alcoholic asked you for a drink, would you be loving him if you gave him a bottle? No, of course not. Giving him alcohol may be submissive to his will, but it wouldn't be in his best interests, and therefore, it wouldn't be honoring to the Lord.

In the same way, if a demanding, abusive, manipulative person commanded you to submit, would you be loving him if you gave in to him? No. The loving thing would be to confront his behavior and help him take steps toward self-control, responsibility, and kindness. Submitting and obeying out of fear is understandable, but it isn't obeying God, and it isn't loving the abusive person because it isn't what is best for him.

Paul encouraged his readers, "Love must be sincere" (Romans 12:9). Don't cower in fear as you obey an abusive person and then call it love. Genuine love is strong enough to speak the truth and do what is best for someone else, even if he doesn't like it. Genuine love also seeks wisdom to make sure you are doing the right thing, not becoming a doormat or compulsively fixing problems because you are afraid, and conversely, not refusing to help because you are angry.

Responding to a Fool

A set of passages in the book of Proverbs can be applied to setting boundaries in abusive relationships. Many of the proverbs talk about wisdom and foolishness. A fool is someone who is stubborn and demands his own way, even when that hurts other people and himself. Here is a small sample of passages:

- "Fools mock at making amends for sin, but goodwill is found among the upright" (14:9). Foolish people won't admit they are wrong.

- "A fool finds no pleasure in understanding but delights in airing his own opinions" (18:2). Foolish people don't listen to others, but they insist that we listen to them.

- "A fool gives full vent to his anger, but a wise man keeps himself under control" (29:11). Foolish people sometimes explode in rage and use their anger to intimidate others.

- "A wicked messenger falls into trouble, but a trustworthy envoy brings healing" (13:17). Foolish people say things that hurt others instead of healing them.

How should we respond to foolish people? Two proverbs seem to contradict each other, but they indicate that we need to be wise and selective in our approach. "Do not answer a fool according to his folly, or you will be like him yourself. Answer a fool according to his folly, or he will be wise in his own eyes" (26:4-5). Sometimes we need to be silent and not get into an argument with a foolish person, but at other times we need to speak boldly and clearly to refute him. Knowing the difference requires wisdom.

"He who walks with the wise grows wise, but a companion of fools suffers harm" (13:20). If we spend too much time around foolish people, we inevitably will be hurt, but if we choose to spend time with loving, kind, and wise people, we will become like them.

Are we to forgive those who have hurt us and who continue to try to control us? Yes, God commands us to forgive them. Should we trust them? Not necessarily. Forgiveness and trust are separate issues. We are commanded to forgive, but we are never commanded to trust untrustworthy people. Trust must be earned by kind, respectful, consistent behavior. To trust those who haven't proven they are trustworthy would be foolish.

When we begin to set boundaries, we often feel tremendous guilt and confusion. Abusive or manipulative people may tell us we are being selfish for setting boundaries, and we may be tempted to cave in and go back to the old ways. Setting boundaries—and sticking with them— is being obedient to God to live according to our strong, new identity in Christ, and it sustains and nurtures that new identity. In addition, our honesty and strength provide the best opportunities for abusive people to change and for love to grow. Our willingness to speak the

truth, set boundaries, and administer consequences creates a new environment of integrity, and it gives others an opportunity to repent. We
can't know if they will respond positively. We can only be strong and
offer that opportunity.

Some Christian leaders have a narrow view of the subject of a wife's
submission. We need to put the verses on submission into a larger
context of the right of self-protection, the true nature of love, and the
admonitions to respond appropriately and wisely to foolish people.
These insights help us set good boundaries.

What You Can Say to Him

In some cases, the last thing an abused woman should do is march
into the living room and confront her husband. If he has shown an explosive, reactive nature, she should
be wise and circumspect in her
actions. I'm not saying she should
remain in the situation and not
take steps to change it, but she
should be careful not to expose
herself to more violence and
abuse. If this happens in a dating
relationship, my best advice is for
her to get out now and run from
it as fast as she can.

> Courage is rightly
> esteemed the first of human
> qualities because, as has
> been said, it is the quality
> which guarantees all others.
> WINSTON CHURCHILL

She needs to find a competent, skilled person to help her take steps
toward resolution. This person isn't just a nice friend or a Christian
who knows the Bible. Her situation can be dangerous, and it usually
requires a professional.

The counselor or pastor will help chart a course of action, including steps to protect the abused woman and confront the problem in a
way that offers a path of hope for both people. This helper also may be

present in one or more conversations with the abusive man. The police or an attorney may also be brought in to protect and advise her.

Earlier in the book, I suggested using a template for conversations: *I feel, I want, I will.* When talking with an abusive person, however, don't express your feelings because he will use them against you. Instead, begin with a clear statement of what you want and then what you are willing to do to move forward in the relationship.

These things are not necessarily easy to determine. Many women need help clarifying what they want. They often focus on particulars instead of the big issues of building trust and the process of pursuing reconciliation. In most cases, I advise women to say, "I want a relationship based on trust and respect. Right now, we don't have that, but I'm willing to take steps toward that if you're willing too." Don't expect him to repent immediately! And don't look only at his words. His actions reveal his true beliefs.

We have a tendency to respond to stressful conversations in the same way over and over again. If we take a good look at our most difficult conversations, we probably see a very clear pattern. Author and counselor Jeff VanVonderen warns people against "getting big" or "getting little." The goal in any painful conversation is "stay who we are."

People get big when they lean forward, raise their voices, give menacing looks, wag their finger in the person's face, and demand compliance. Have you been the recipient of any of these maneuvers? Have you used them to get your way? The goal for these people is to intimidate other people, to get them to back down, and to win at all costs.

We get little when we face an intimidating person (or someone who is only speaking the truth in a way that is calm but that we perceive as intimidating) and slink down in our chairs, look down or away, whisper instead of speaking up, and mumble nonsense rather than staying on the subject. The goal of acting this way is to get the conversation over as quickly as possible by giving in and to avoid antagonizing the other person and escalating the conflict.

Many of us act as if we're insane—we keep doing the same thing over and over again but hope the results will be different next time. That's magical thinking, and it isn't rooted in reality. We can begin to improve our communication in these situations by analyzing our normal pattern of responding in difficult conversations. Do we get big or get little? Some of us get big with those who we feel are less powerful than us, like our children, but we get little in conflict with those we perceive as more powerful than us, like our parents, spouse, or boss.

After we've been honest about our usual behavior, we have a benchmark for change. I suggest that women role-play their next conversation and practice staying who they are in the conversation. If they usually get big, they can make a conscious choice to lower their voices, sit back, and ask questions without jumping in to give their opinions. Their goal is for the other person to feel valued and heard, not to win at all costs.

And if they normally get little, they can envision themselves sitting up straight, giving eye contact, and speaking the truth in a calm, measured voice. When the intimidating person tries to blow them away, they can say, "No, you need to hear what I'm saying." At first, the intimidating person won't believe she's serious. Surely, he thinks, she'll buckle under just a little more anger. After all, that's what she's done before. She may need to say, "You need to know that things have changed. I'm not going to cave in like I used to. I want a real relationship, not one based on your power and my compliance. I hope you want that too, but it's going to take adjustments for both of us."

Don't expect to feel completely comfortable when you change the way you respond in the most threatening situations in your life! This kind of change doesn't come easily. You'll probably feel insecure, guilty, and confused. It's crucial to have a mature friend or a counselor to help you prepare for this important shift in communication and help you understand that courage can overcome all the fears and doubts you'll face. After a few times, though, you'll realize you can do it. Change won't come easily for him either. At first, he won't believe you mean business, and when you persist, he may redouble his efforts to intimidate you. Be ready and stay strong.

Self-perception isn't optional in difficult relationships. We simply must look closely at the patterns of our thoughts, feelings, and actions so we can make necessary changes. If we aren't ruthlessly honest with ourselves and one other person, we'll almost certainly stay stuck in the same destructive patterns that have served us so poorly for so long.

Women in these relationships have suffered major damage to their hearts and minds, so even if the abusive men respond quickly or positively, the women need time and attention to grieve the losses they've endured and to forgive the offender as much and as soon as they can. Forgiveness isn't merely a pleasant feeling. It's a choice; the feelings will follow sooner or later.

Abused women have no guarantee that their honesty and offers of reconciliation will be accepted. All a woman can do is make the offer and let her man respond. If he says yes, the couple can begin traveling the long, bumpy road of rebuilding the relationship. If they do, they may well find more love and peace than ever before. They will face plenty of detours and setbacks, so women need to be ready for every obstacle along the way.

Through it all, Christ has promised His presence, power, and empathy. He understands because He was rejected and abused. He cares because He loves the outcasts and the brokenhearted. And He offers a path of peace for anyone who is willing to take His hand. He promises us that!

In the Word: Chapter Seven Application

This chapter may have been difficult for you to read. It was a hard chapter to write. I have spoken with numerous women who have shared horrific details about living for years in abusive relationships. The stories break my heart because they should never have happened. In this closing section, I want to take a deeper look at abuse and how to respond biblically.

First, let's take a snapshot of abuse and the persons involved. *Domestic violence* is the name given to a situation where a strong partner (usually the male, but not always) abuses the weaker one (usually the woman, but not always). This abuse can be physical, sexual, verbal, and emotional. The abuser will continue to abuse because he is getting what he wants as a result of the abuse—control and manipulation of the other spouse.

A codependent person is a spouse who is addicted to a bad or abusive relationship. She excuses, denies, minimizes, and ultimately supports her spouse's violence. Keep in mind that *both* partners are addicted to this terrible dance, and the concerted efforts of many others will be necessary to help them break and overcome this vicious cycle.

A codependent, abusive cycle can literally kill the victim or at the very least cause great harm. She is likely to justify her part by believing that she and the relationship will die if she stands up to the violence (because of his rage against her or because of the loss of the relationship). In her mind, trying to manage and live with the abuse is better than risking a greater loss by losing the man she may still love.

Clearing Away Some Confusion

Spousal abuse is not something a woman can manage and live with. It will escalate until someone is hurt deeply or even killed. It will also be passed on to the children, who are watching a corrupted model and learning to abuse or be abused when they become adults.

Abuse and violence have no place in the family. They must end immediately. The abuser must be stopped, or the victim must leave the relationship until the abuser has changed. (This doesn't automatically mean divorce, but it could entail a substantial time of separation.) Even though either path is scary and carries no guarantees, the key is doing whatever is necessary to *stop the violence now!*

In her exposition on violence in *The Soul Care Bible*, Leslie Vernick explicates a fivefold path that all victims of violence should study and take to heart to begin a new cycle of action in the face of violence.

1. Protect yourself from violent people. Proverbs 27:12 says, "The prudent see danger and take refuge." You have the right—even the duty, for the sake of your children and the future of your marriage—to set firm boundaries that make no allowance for violence from your spouse. The best outcome of your attempts to manage the situation would entail shifting to a position that shows him that godly management never includes violence. The relationship addict has no healthy boundaries in place. A wise woman de-escalates any fighting without caving in to coercive demands, and if she can't, she simply leaves. Never forget this foundational truth—you have the right and duty to protect yourself and your children from violence.

2. Expose the deeds done in darkness. Ephesians 5:11 states that believers "have nothing to do with the fruitless deeds of darkness, but rather expose them." Again, this reinforces the summons out of codependency, which aligns with darkness, and into the light. Exposure here puts a whole new contingency in place—the abuser suffers pain for his evil deeds instead of getting what he wants.

The exposure must be done carefully, and it must naturally lead to the two of you involving others. Simply naming violence for what it is and letting the abuser know it is no longer acceptable will go a long way to changing the equation between you two. But then you will need to add a good friend, pastor, or accountability partner to show your measured firmness. Including the police may be necessary if immediate safety is a concern due to his defensiveness and refusal to take counsel.

3. Always speak the truth in love. Ephesians 4:14-15 helps us identify our goal. "We will no longer be infants, tossed back and forth by the waves, and blown here and there by every wind of teaching and by the cunning and craftiness of men in their deceitful scheming. Instead, speaking the truth in love, we will in all things grow up into him who is the Head, that is, Christ." The cycle of abuse and codependences is crafty and evil.

We learn some good news: In Christ we are enabled to grow out of that vicious cycle and into something new and holy! We learn that truth without love is ultimately harsh and breaks down relationships, while love without truth sets no boundaries at all and allows all manner of sin to escalate and contaminate.

Leslie notes that this is the way to overcome evil—not with a counterattack that creates more evil, but by the good that comes from speaking the truth in love and naming violence and threats for the evil that they are. Eventually, you (or a therapist or a pastor) can speak to him about his fears of losing you if he doesn't control you. You can also point out that further abuse will actually cause you to leave. These steps can help him take the risk of letting love and respect guide the relationship.

4. *Allow violent people to experience the consequences of their actions.* Proverbs 19:19 reveals, "A hot-tempered man must pay the penalty; if you rescue him, you will have to do it again." The relationship addict is the consummate rescuer—she deflects and helps the abuser avoid the necessary consequences of his wrath and violence. This behavior cycles over and over again until one person leaves or dies.

If he can continue to manipulate you in fear, he will never stop using violence or the threat of it to control you. But if you leave home as he escalates to violence, or if he lands in jail for violent behavior, he will quickly learn that his abuse comes at a very high price. For a short time, this price will seem higher to you than the price of your various ineffective rescue and management strategies. But you must stick with it for a measured time as the abuser rages to keep the cycle in place.

5. *Finally, be gracious to an enemy.*

> Do not take revenge, my friends, but leave room for God's wrath, for it is written: "It is mine to avenge; I will repay," says the Lord. On the contrary: "If your enemy is hungry, feed him; if he is thirsty, give him something to drink. In doing this, you will heap burning coals on his head."

Do not be overcome by evil, but overcome evil with good
(Romans 12:19-21).

By maintaining an attitude of love and not repaying evil for evil,
you will prick his conscience, and through that tiny opening the Holy
Spirit will enter and agitate your husband about his sin. By remaining
gracious, kind, and caring—even as you stick to your new boundaries unwaveringly—you show the one you love that you are not his
enemy and that you truly love him and want the relationship to survive. Your real enemies—the things both of you can join together and
fight during the end stage of this transformation—are his sinful violence and your codependence.

Only God working in us is able to empower us to break out of this
powerful cycle. In our own strength alone, we are too overcome by our
fear or rage to be effective this way. We must pray our way through all
five steps if we are to give our men a fighting chance to leave behind
the behavior they secretly hate somewhere inside.

Have a Plan to Keep You and Your Children Safe

If you or someone you love is in an abusive relationship, make a
plan of escape and find a safe place to stay to be away from violence.
Many communities have shelters that will house needy women and
their children for several days. If you have family nearby who can provide a place of refuge, all the better.

The plan will include having a suitcase packed with the necessary
clothes and family care items, and tucking it away in your car or at
a safe house in advance. Remember, you have committed to stop the
violence regardless of how disruptive this may be to the family routine.
The abuser may break things in the house or rage on by himself, but you
must not allow you and your children to be victims of that rage.

Do not allow any quick repentance, pleas for forgiveness, or tears
to dissuade you from going away for a while. The pattern of abuse

and codependence often includes repeated shortcuts to reconciliation that include confession and tearful promises that the abuse will never happen again. If you have believed that in the past, stop and ask God what the way of wisdom is now. If quick repentance has always melted your heart in the past, you must act differently now. The violence will not stop until you are able to put all five steps into practice.

Reflection Questions

1. After reading this chapter, would you say that your current relationship is abusive? If so, what decisions do you need to make in order to stop the violence?

2. If you are currently being abused, the violence must stop now. First, you must begin with establishing a safety plan. Whom can you call today to help you develop and execute this plan? Make a secret list of shelters in your area that provide safe havens if you need to leave your home. If you need to locate a licensed therapist in your area, go to www.ecounseling.com or call 1-866-COUNSEL for a referral.

3. If you are not currently in an emotionally or physically abusive relationship, have you been hurt or caused hurt in your relationship in any way? If so, what can you do today to make amends, reconcile, and restore the relationship?

8 My Desires and Fantasies

We are destined to misunderstand the story we find ourselves in.

G.K. CHESTERTON

I WISH. . .

What do you wish for? What do you wish about?

Each of us lives in a story, and we imagine how we would like it to unfold. But most women make one of two errors when they picture the future. They envision outcomes that are either too little or too big. We need Goldilocks dreams that are just the right size.

Sarah began, "Julie, I've listened to people talk about God fulfilling our dreams, but I'm confused. For a long time, I haven't really had any dreams. For 12 years, I lived with an abusive alcoholic. Oh, at our wedding I was like any other bride, full of anticipation about the future. But soon his drinking escalated into using cocaine, and he became a selfish tyrant. I lived under the cloud of his addiction for a long, long time. During all those years, my hopes and dreams were pulverized. Usually my goal each day was just to survive—you know, to avoid falling apart."

I told her, "I'm sorry you were hurt so badly."

Sarah nodded, and then she continued her saga. "But that's only half of the story. In one sense, my dreams were shattered, but in my mind, I created a fantasy world of the purest joys. Day after day, I thought about a strikingly handsome knight on a white horse riding to my rescue. Sometimes I'd have thoughts about a man at church who looked nice, but I didn't even know him. He could have been an addict too for all I knew!" She laughed at herself and then explained, "My real life was a disaster, but my thoughts drifted each day to a fairy-tale land where a handsome prince passionately loved me. I get so angry when I look at real life and things aren't going my way, but half the time, I don't even know what I would want anyway." Sarah paused for a second and asked, "Julie, do you think I'm crazy?"

Hurts and Dreams

Hurts that haven't healed inevitably distort our desires. Prolonged disappointment can lead to nagging and persistent discouragement, which rob us of hope that our lives will ever be pleasant or meaningful. Like a car with four flat tires, we may have a lot of things going for us, but we can't move an inch. Every day is devoted to making it through one more hour, one more meal, one more encounter with people we should love but who produce fear in us. Gradually, joy and spontaneity evaporate into thin air, and the circle of life is reduced to a dot.

> When one door of happiness closes, another opens; but often we look so long at the closed door that we do not see the one which has been opened for us.
>
> HELEN KELLER

But unresolved pain can also lead to an opposite reaction. Instead of giving up in hopelessness, we become defiant. We tell ourselves, *I'm never going to let anybody hurt me again, and I'm going to get all I can out of the people around me.* We're not passive; we're demanding, and we let everyone know that we aren't going to be happy unless they give us what we want! Like little Chihuahuas, we bark at our husbands, our children, the postman, the neighboring dog, and anyone else who dares to cross our paths.

And some of us are like my friend Sarah, vacillating between these two extremes, crushed and hopeless one moment and demanding the next. We drive ourselves (and everybody around us) crazy.

And others of us just wish for something else...or more.

Nothing Wrong with Desires

God made us with a tremendous capacity for creativity. In fact, I believe that most of us have far more creative energy than we use. It's there inside us, waiting to be tapped. Throughout the Scriptures, we see men and women longing for more. They saw needs, and they dove in to meet those needs. They saw injustice, and they moved heaven and earth to right the

> The man's desire is for the woman; but the woman's desire is rarely other than for the desire of the man.
> SAMUEL TAYLOR COLERIDGE

wrongs that hurt people. The longing for more isn't necessarily evil or sinful. But we have to be careful to avoid letting the ways of the world determine our desires.

God made women with intrinsic beauty, but oh my, we can become obsessed with our looks instead of enjoying the beauty God put in us and around us. God wants us to raise our children to be strong, confident, and independent, but too many of us want our kids' success to be a reflection of our skill as parents. It's all about us, not them! God gives us so much to enjoy, but too often, our hearts become enamored with the gifts of money, clothes, vacations, cars, houses, and jewelry, and we don't get around to thanking the Giver.

We shouldn't be afraid of our desires, but we need to carefully consider where they are leading us. Marketers and advertisers try to convince us that we can't possibly be happy unless we have this product or that service. The underlying message is that we need those things so we can look more beautiful or successful than some other person, whoever she may be.

Fantasy World

Redbook conducted a national survey of women to ask them about secrets they keep from their husbands and boyfriends, including their most common and most powerful fantasies. Some of the responses are funny, and some are sad.

> I try to stay focused on my life and do try not to be brought into the Hollywood fantasy.
>
> ACTRESS JENNIFER CONNELLY

1. Everything we buy for ourselves—shoes, a skirt, even just stuff from the drugstore—really costs 20 percent more than we tell you it did.

2. We actually think about sex—with you!—a lot.

3. We're just as nervous about commitment as you are.

4. We may be modern and independent, but we still want you to be "the man."

5. Our ex-boyfriends were not completely terrible in bed.

6. We're scared that we'll turn into our mothers.

7. We want you to be jealous—but just a little bit.

8. Yes, we fantasize about hot celebrity guys, but that doesn't mean we want you to be them.

9. We tell our girlfriends more than we admit to you (but less than you fear).

10. We really do notice and appreciate all the chores you do.

11. We love you with all our hearts, but we still get wistful about the fact that we'll never feel that falling-in-love sizzle and spark again.[1]

When I read this list, a few observations jump out. We women want to feel alive in every way, and we want our men to understand that our desires (most of them, anyway) aren't a threat to them at all. In fact, many of our desires focus on them. We long for richer, stronger, more intimate relationships with the men we love. If they understood that, they'd relax more, be less defensive and doubtful, and enjoy us a lot more. But then, maybe we need to do a better job of relieving their fears.

Sex certainly isn't the only desire in a woman's life, but it's important—and it becomes an even more powerful fantasy if our sex life isn't what it should be. A recent survey conducted by Families.com found these statistics:

- 53 percent admitted to having thoughts of cheating.
- 34 percent confessed to having cheated.
- 58 percent admitted they fantasize about men other than their husbands, such as coworkers, deliverymen, and other women's husbands.
- The top three celebrities women admitted having crushes on were George Clooney, Tom Brady, and Barack Obama.[2]

As this survey indicates, some women don't stop with just daydreaming about having sex with other men. They actually do it. And many women today are involved in what used to be a man's problem: pornography. An article published in *Today's Christian Women* revealed that 17 percent of women today, including Christian women, struggle with an addiction to pornography. This figure parallels a study conducted by Zogby International indicating the number of women who believe they can find sexual fulfillment on the Internet. At first, women prefer cybersex and chat rooms more than simply pictures and stories because they value companionship, but soon, they use both. Engaging in pornography stimulates chemicals in the brain that closely approximate the impact of cocaine. The instant euphoria is addictive, but loneliness returns, leaving women craving more stimulation.[3]

Desires and dreams are part of being a human being. They are powerful forces that can be used to create or destroy. We need to be careful to analyze our desires so that they produce good in our lives instead of destruction.

Alignment

I believe we are most fulfilled when we align our desires with God and with our husbands. Does God have a dream for us? He certainly does! He wants us to enjoy Him and His plan to the fullest. Jesus said He came to give us abundant life. Not an easy life, but one that is full of love and purpose. God wants us to care for Him more than anything else in the world. Does this kind of devotion to God make us sour and dour? Not at all! As we get closer to Him, we know Him better, and we find Him to be even more beautiful. We find life's greatest delights when our desires are aligned with His. Author and pastor John Piper has often said, "God is most honored when we are most satisfied in Him." By learning to be completely satisfied in God and not in the deceptive pleasures of our culture, we shape our dreams and can fulfill them.

In his brilliant book *The Call,* author Os Guinness defines our spiritual calling as "the truth that God calls us to himself so decisively that everything we are, everything we do, and everything we have is invested with a special devotion and dynamism lived out as a response to his summons and service."[4] Where do we find maximum fulfillment? Right in the center of God's calling. What fills our lives with delight? Walking each day with the One who loves us, directs us, and uses us to touch others' lives.

We can also align our desires with our husbands' deepest longings. And yes, they undoubtedly have some! That statement doesn't imply that we no longer have our own dreams and desires. Alignment is the coordination of two independent souls who find common interests in their love for each other. Men are just as susceptible to run off into either of the two ditches of desires as we are. Some of them had high hopes when they first met their future wives, but years of hard work and deep disappointments have left them feeling empty and alone. Like many of us, their goal each day is to survive and provide for the family. But others have responded to disappointments by seeking joys from anything and anyone. They may devote themselves to fishing or other hobbies, or they may pursue "false intimacies" of pornography or adultery. One of the biggest acts of love we can show our men is to tenderly help them rediscover dreams that may have been buried for many years.

I know a couple now in their sixties who basically coexisted for the middle years of their marriage. At first, she had high hopes of intimacy and partnership, but he seemed to be more committed to his work than to her. When she tried to talk to him about it, he always became defensive and reminded her that their lifestyle was based on the long hours he spent at the factory, where he worked as a midlevel manager. Only a few years ago, though, both of them had a spiritual awakening. In a short time, they began talking about things they had avoided for years. They found common ground, and their love deepened. When she learned she had cancer, their love for each other grew even stronger. (She said she shudders to think of what it would have been like if she'd gotten sick when they were emotionally and spiritually estranged.) Today, he's retired, and they work together through a ministry of their church to care for homeless people. "I wish we'd found this kind of partnership years ago," she told me with a wistful smile. "But this is wonderful. We enjoy each other more now than ever."

Waiting on God

The Bible frequently encourages us to "wait on the Lord." That has probably never been easy to do, but in our instant culture, it's really hard—at least for me! We want what we want, and we want it now. Every new electronic device is designed to give us more information and quicker contacts with people than ever before. Communication and information technology has progressed at an astounding rate in just a few short years. But God doesn't always operate according to our lightning-quick timetable. To Him, waiting is part of the process of learning important lessons—ones we can't acquire any other way. Demanding an instant solution to every problem and an immediate fulfillment of every desire keeps us from learning from God's curriculum. We need to discover that aligning our desires with God's purposes often involves the discipline of waiting.

> Patience is waiting. Not passively waiting. That is laziness. But to keep going when the going is hard and slow—that is patience.

God may delay His answers in order to purify our hearts, or He may need to work in someone else's heart before He answers. Sometimes He delays to see if we're willing to trust Him and cling to Him without giving up during the long wait. And sometimes He's orchestrating different circumstances so the impact is most powerful when we finally see His answer. Isaiah says, "Those who hope in the LORD will renew their strength. They will soar on wings like eagles; they will run and not grow weary, they will walk and not be faint" (Isaiah 40:31).

Pastor Chuck Swindoll says that waiting is the most difficult task for believers. I think he's right. Everything in us wants quick solutions. After all, we're used to even the most complex relational, emotional, or health-related difficulty being resolved by the end of a television program or movie. The solutions to our problems shouldn't take any longer than that! God, though, uses waiting in powerful and positive ways—if we'll trust Him.

I've wanted quick solutions just like everybody else, and though it's not easy, I now try to remind myself of an important lesson. Instead of becoming angry with God because He doesn't do what I want as quickly as I want Him to do it, I look to Him and ask, *Lord, what is this waiting about? Do You want to teach me something?* And usually He does. I need to listen, reflect, and take steps to obey as He directs me. I'm making progress in learning to wait, but I'm afraid I have much more to learn.

I love the way one of the psalms describes waiting for the Lord. The writer compares us to the watchmen who stand guard at night on the walls of the city. During the night, enemies can sneak up on them. The guards are looking carefully, and they long for the sun to come up so they can see what's really going on. Will the sun come up? Of course. That's what they're counting on. The psalmist says we can have the same certainty. Just as the soldiers are sure the sun will come up, we can be sure God will come through for us—when it's time.

> I wait for the Lord, my soul waits,
> 　　and in his word I put my hope.
> My soul waits for the Lord
> 　　more than watchmen wait for the morning,
> 　　more than watchmen wait for the morning.
> O Israel, put your hope in the Lord,
> 　　for with the Lord is unfailing love
> 　　and with him is full redemption (Psalm 130:5-7).

When our desires, God's desires, and our husbands' desires are aligned, amazing things happen. We experience more joy and love, and many of the conflicts in our hearts and our relationships subside. In place of despair or demands, we find that most attractive trait of Christian character: thankfulness.

I love Paul's little letter to the Philippians. It's a thank-you note for their generosity in helping to fund his ministry. Near the end of his letter, he almost explodes with this heartfelt advice:

> Rejoice in the Lord always. I will say it again: Rejoice! Let your gentleness be evident to all. The Lord is near. Do not be anxious about anything, but in everything, by prayer and petition, with thanksgiving, present your requests to God. And the peace of God, which transcends all understanding, will guard your hearts and your minds in Christ Jesus (Philippians 4:4-7).

These people weren't deciding which condo to use this weekend. They lived in a small Roman colony on the coast of Greece. They were just normal people who were trying to walk with God and make a difference in the world. Paul reminded them that God's presence was with them all day every day. With His care and direction, they could relax, give thanks, and trust Him to lead them as they prayed. The result would be an overwhelming sense of God's peace—the exact opposite of hopelessness or demands.

Are your desires, God's desires, and your husband's desires all aligned? Most of us could use a little work on that! As we mature in our walks with Christ, we open our hearts to let Him change us from the inside out. The light of His grace reaches into our deepest desires, enflames the ones that are noble and pure, and changes the others. This process takes time and energy, but if we trust God's Spirit, He'll do an amazing work in us.

What You Can Say to Him

The best thing some of us can do is stop saying things to our men about our desires. We've already said way too much! They feel as if we've demanded the moon, and our harping has made them feel inadequate and alone. But others of us haven't expressed a desire to our husbands in years. We've avoided any hint of conflict, and we're sure that they would be upset if we voiced even a meek and mild preference. First, we need to take stock of our hearts and our communication: What are our deepest desires, and how are we communicating them? Are we leaning toward either extreme of being demanding or emotionally numb?

Also, before we figure out what to say to our husbands, we may need to talk to God about how well our desires align with His purposes for our lives. Some of us (or maybe *all* of us) need to make some adjustments. Look in the Scriptures—what are the things that thrill God? What are the things that break His heart? When we answer those questions, we can then ask how much those things thrill us and break our hearts too.

After some rigorous self-analysis, a pinch of confession, and a dollop of repentance, we can think about what we want to say to our men. I suggest we consider these elements:

1. "I'm learning to match my desires with God's dream for me. Here's what I'm learning, and here are some changes I need to make." Describe the process you've gone through to come to this insight about yourself.

2. If you've been demanding or uncaring about your man's desires, tell him you're sorry. And mean it.

3. Invite your man to share his desires with you. They may be so buried that he doesn't even know what they are, but they may be as fresh as this morning's hopes and disappointments.

4. Share your vision for what alignment with God and your husband might look like. You don't need to have all the answers at this point. Just explain that you're in the process of figuring out these things, and let him participate in the conversation. If you don't have a shared dream instantly on the tip of your tongue, don't despair. Uncovering a vision

that is meaningful to both of you is part of the adventure
in your relationship.

5. Make a commitment to keep talking about your dreams,
his dreams, and your shared dreams. Don't let this be a
one-time conversation. Remember, God made us to be
dreamers, full of hope and energy to try creative things,
and relationships are most fulfilling when you can find
common interests to pursue together.

When we uncover our own desires and trust God to guide us so our
dreams match His dreams for us, we are on our way to true fulfillment.
We will be genuinely interested in our husbands' deepest dreams, and
maybe we can find something to do together that thrills both of us.

In the Word: Chapter Eight Application

We are all familiar with Disney World and their organizational theme,
"Where Dreams Come True." We've heard Jiminy Cricket sing "When
You Wish upon a Star." Wouldn't that be nice if every wish really did
come true? (Actually, if you've ever been to Disney World with a child,
you could make a strong case that the song is telling the truth!)

As we discussed in this chapter, all women have desires, wishes,
and dreams. Problems arise, however, when these desires become the
foundation for a fantasy world you choose to live in. In this section, I
want to focus on how to make your desires, wishes, and dreams align
with God's vision for your life.

Hurts and Dreams

Take a look at the following verses from the book of Psalms:

- "The righteous cry out, and the LORD hears them; he delivers them from all their troubles. The LORD is close to the brokenhearted and saves those who are crushed in spirit. A righteous man may have many troubles, but the LORD delivers him from them all; he protects all his bones, not one of them will be broken" (Psalm 34:17-20).

- "He heals the brokenhearted and binds up their wounds" (Psalm 147:3).

- "'What gain is there in my destruction, in my going down into the pit? Will the dust praise you? Will it proclaim your faithfulness? Hear, O LORD, and be merciful to me; O LORD, be my help.' You turned my wailing into dancing; you removed my sackcloth and clothed me with joy, that my heart may sing to you and not be silent. O LORD my God, I will give you thanks forever" (Psalm 30:9-12).

You've probably heard people say that you always have a choice when you are hurt. You can become *bitter*, or you can become *better*. When you are hurt, the natural response is to build a wall around your heart and emotions and to vow never to experience that kind of pain again. Depression and bitterness begin to form in your heart and start you on a path of isolation and destruction. David clearly saw his human ability to go down this road when he realized, "What gain is there in my destruction, in my going down into the pit?"

You gain nothing when you harbor bitterness in your heart. In fact, *you* are the only one who suffers when bitterness takes hold. Bitterness will distort your view of God's dream for your life, cause you to doubt God's provision, and discourage you from seeking the truth. It will stop you from experiencing joy and fulfillment in the relationships you cherish most in life. And unresolved hurt almost always leads to a bitter spirit!

The Fantasy World

Midway through this chapter we mentioned some of the fantasies many women have. Some were funny and harmless. Others were more serious and could easily lead to sinful outcomes. To guard against acting out sinful fantasies, we must first recognize the battle going on in the spiritual realm for control over our thought life. In one of Paul's most personal letters, he writes this to the church in Corinth:

> For though we live in the world, we do not wage war as the world does. The weapons we fight with are not the weapons of the world. On the contrary, they have divine power to demolish strongholds. We demolish arguments and every pretension that sets itself up against the knowledge of God, and we take captive every thought to make it obedient to Christ (2 Corinthians 10:3-5).

Paul also addresses spiritual warfare in his letter to the church at Ephesus: "For our struggle is not against flesh and blood, but against the rulers, against the authorities, against the powers of this dark world and against the spiritual forces of evil in the heavenly realms" (Ephesians 6:12).

Our enemy is Satan. First Peter 5:8 says, "Be self-controlled and alert. Your enemy the devil prowls around like a roaring lion looking for someone to devour." He would love nothing more than to destroy you and those you love. You must guard your mind and your fantasies at all times.

Alignment

"Finally, brothers, whatever is true, whatever is noble, whatever is right, whatever is pure, whatever is lovely, whatever is admirable—if anything is excellent or praiseworthy—think about such things" (Philippians 4:8). You cannot control what thoughts or fantasies pop into your mind, but you can control whether they stay there. As we saw in this chapter, you will find life's greatest delights when your desires are aligned with God's desires for your life.

You may be thinking, *Okay, Julie, how do I go about aligning myself with God's will?* One of my favorite passages in the Bible is found in the book of Proverbs:

> Trust in the LORD with all your heart and lean not on your own understanding; in all your ways acknowledge him, and he will make your paths straight. Do not be wise in your own eyes; fear the LORD and shun evil. This will bring health to your body and nourishment to your bones (Proverbs 3:5-8).

You see, it's not about you. It's all about God and trusting Him! Aligning with God involves reading, studying, meditating, and memorizing His Word daily. It's about praying and asking for wisdom and guidance. "If any of you lacks wisdom, he should ask God, who gives generously to all without finding fault, and it will be given to him" (James 1:5).

When you are in alignment with God and His will for your life, you will see things clearly. You will become more like Him in your daily actions and your reactions to the circumstances around you. He doesn't promise that life will be easy or trouble free, but He does promise to lead you through.

Waiting on the Lord

Let's take a look at what the Bible says about waiting on God:

- "Do you not know? Have you not heard? The LORD is the everlasting God, the Creator of the ends of the earth. He will not grow tired or weary, and his understanding no one can fathom. He gives strength to the weary and increases the power of the weak. Even youths grow tired and weary, and young men stumble and fall; but those who hope in the LORD will renew their strength. They will soar on wings like eagles; they will run and not grow weary, they will walk and not be faint" (Isaiah 40:28-31).

- "Find rest, O my soul, in God alone; my hope comes from him" (Psalm 62:5).

- "We wait in hope for the LORD; he is our help and our shield" (Psalm 33:20).

- "I waited patiently for the LORD; he turned to me and heard my cry. He lifted me out of the slimy pit, out of the mud and mire; he set my feet on a rock and gave me a firm place to stand. He put a new song in my mouth, a hymn of praise to our God. Many will see and fear and put their trust in the LORD" (Psalm 40:1-3).

Fall is one of my favorite seasons. I live at the foot of the Blue Ridge Mountains in Virginia, and the beautiful colors on the leaves all around amaze me every year. In life, we have seasons too—a season of joy when a new baby is born, a season of pain when a loved one passes away. "There is a time for everything, and a season for every activity under heaven" (Ecclesiastes 3:1). God's will unfolds through the seasons of a person's life.

Esther's life is a perfect example. A young girl with plans of her own suddenly finds herself in the king's court, preparing to be presented as a possible replacement for the former queen, who had been banished from royalty. When Esther is chosen to be queen, she can't help but wonder what purpose God had for her life. I love Mordecai's response to Esther when she discusses her confusion with him: "For if you remain silent at this time, relief and deliverance for the Jews will arise from another place, but you and your father's family will perish. And who knows but that you have come to royal position for such a time as this?" (Esther 4:14). Wow!

As the story goes on, we learn that as a result of Esther's courage, her people's lives were saved. Esther had questioned her position. She had struggled with understanding God's will. Yet she stood firm and believed that God was sovereign.

Learn to trust God and wait on His perfect timing. His will is never instantaneous. It always includes a time of preparation and teaching. Following Him is a lifelong journey of experiences, both happy and sad, that accomplish the plan He has for each of us. And it's a plan worth waiting for—greater than we could ever imagine!

Reflection Questions

1. Have you ever felt discouraged because the marriage or dating relationship you dreamed about as a little girl differs from your current situation? Have you ever taken the time to analyze the differences in light of God's Word?

2. Do you struggle in your thought life? Are impure desires and fantasies hard to control? If these fantasies were fulfilled and acted out, how would they impact your marriage or dating relationship?

3. What choices can you make today to stand against Satan in the battle for your mind? How can you begin to align with God and His desire for your life and your marriage or dating relationship?

I'm not telling him about. . .

9 How I Feel About Our Differing Parenting Styles

Folly is bound in the heart of a child, but the rod of discipline will drive it far from him.

PROVERBS 22:15

MY DAUGHTER, MEGAN, NEEDS TO BE AFFIRMED. She feels loved with a simple "I love you" text message or phone call from Tim or me when one of us is out of town. Zach, on the other hand, is a snuggler. He loves physical touch. He enjoys wrestling with Tim or lying on the couch with me. He loves and needs time and affection. Tim and I learned the different ways Megan and Zach give and receive love. We also realized that we needed to adjust our parenting strategies to fit each child so that they didn't feel unloved by the way we disciplined them.

Counselors, pastors, and other people who regularly talk to parents know that dissimilar approaches to raising children are significant sources of conflict in marriage. One parent is too harsh; the other is too soft. One is too distant; the other is too smothering. Parents don't just come up with their parenting opinions and plans out of thin air. Their perceptions were crafted day by day when they were growing up. And with all that firsthand experience, each parent feels certain he or she is right! With such divergent perspectives on such an important topic, disagreements can quickly escalate into all-out war!

Cyndi and Robert had a wonderful, romantic relationship when they were dating, and when she became pregnant in their third year of marriage, they expected the storybook relationship to get even better. But a few weeks after they brought Ashley home from the hospital, a rift began to appear. Like most babies, Ashley didn't sleep through the night. Cyndi's mother gave her advice about how to help the baby sleep, and Robert's mom gave him exactly the opposite suggestion. The combination of exhaustion, disagreement, and parental pressure (or at least loyalty to each parent's perspective) turned a minor irritation into a cataclysm!

The tension between the unhappy couple lasted for months and then eased a little when Ashley finally started sleeping six or seven hours each night. But the differences in parenting styles didn't vanish in the baby's dreams. As the years went on and two other children entered the family, the couple's differences became sources of constant conflict.

By the time the children were in elementary and junior high school, the walls between Cyndi and Robert kept them isolated, and they used big guns of criticism, nagging, and blame every time one of the children had a problem. Robert accused Cyndi of being too easy on the kids, bailing them out of every problem, and not letting them learn from their mistakes. Cyndi called it love, and she was furious about Robert's lack of empathy and sensitivity for their children's difficulties. The more she perceived him not caring, the more she poured on the attention to rescue them and make up for his lack of affection. The more she bailed them out and lavished excessive attention on them, the more Robert withdrew and demanded that the kids, especially the boys, develop some toughness.

The verbal and emotional warfare between Robert and Cyndi didn't go unnoticed by their parents or their kids. Their parents took sides to defend their own against the "unreasonable" and "destructive" behavior of the spouse, and the kids played their parents like a drum. They learned they could get whatever they wanted from their mother by whining about how their dad didn't love them and was too harsh and demanding.

This family was a mess—a mess that's played out in different ways in countless families around the country. The problems may have different looks and labels, but without the common ground of understanding, couples experience conflict over one of the most important issues in their lives.

Differences Aren't Evil

When we dated our men, the differences between us and them worked to attract us to them and them to us. Somewhere along the way, though, many couples begin to despise the differences they used to admire. Conflicting perspectives, values, and parenting styles can produce explosions of anger and result

> A baby will make love stronger, days shorter, nights longer, bankroll smaller, home happier, clothes shabbier, the past forgotten, and the future worth living for.

in pain and distance. On the other hand, they can also be sources of tremendous creative energy. They are, in many ways, like nuclear power—one force can produce very different results. The key to turning this power into a positive creative force is understanding.

Psychologist David Olson observed the dynamics in families, and he crafted a model of beliefs and behavior that incorporates opposites into a balanced whole.[1] The goal of family relationships, he argues, isn't for everybody to be on the same page and hold the same views about everything, but to understand each other, affirm differences, and find balance between opposing views. Olson uses the metaphor of skiing to describe how a family can find balance and function properly:

> A professional skier smoothly shifts his or her weight from one leg to another, whereas a novice skier tends to emphasize one leg or another. In balanced families, people are able to move in a more fluid manner...whereas unbalanced systems tend to be stuck at one extreme or the other and have a difficult time shifting.[2]

Despising differences accentuates imbalance, but understanding and affirmation can result in far more healthy family relationships, especially in parenting our kids. Two factors that family members must consider when trying to understand and balance their differences are emotional bonding and flexibility in making decisions.

Emotional bonding

Every significant relationship needs to value both ends of the spectrum of emotional bonding: separateness and togetherness. The individuals in a family have their own identities, with personal goals, desires, pursuits, and skills that are different from others'. But the entire family also shares one unique identity as a cohesive whole. The extremes of this continuum, which Robert and Cyndi experienced in spades, are isolation and enmeshment. Robert became so distant and disconnected that he became an outsider in his own home. And Cyndi's smothering style of parenting caused her to lose her role as an authority figure who balanced love with realistic expectations of obedience as she helped children grow into maturity.

Sometimes being alone is entirely appropriate, and sometimes interacting is important. Families can find balance in this area by paying

> Praise your children openly, reprehend them secretly.
> W. CECIL

attention to several factors. For example, personality plays a role. Introverts gain strength and pleasure from time alone. They can enjoy brief forays into the world of interaction, but too much "people time" drains them. On the other hand, extroverts wonder why their "reclusive" family members don't want to hang out more. If they don't understand the difference personality plays in bonding preferences, they can easily communicate disapproval or condemnation instead of acceptance.

Stages of life are also important factors to consider when searching for a balanced approach to emotional bonding. For example, adolescence is a time for children to become independent young adults. In those crucial years, their job is to pull away and carve out their own identity. Parents who insist that their teenagers remain intimately attached to them—looking to the parents for every answer and always choosing to hang out with Mom and Dad—create tremendous tension in the lives of their teens. They follow a recipe for anger and possibly for disaster.

When we understand the way personal preferences and stages of life influence the way we bond with each other, we look for ways to find balance between separateness and togetherness—for each person and for the whole family. We no longer demand compliance with our narrow perceptions of the way things should be. And when everybody in the family grasps this dynamic, we can talk more openly about our desires and needs in this area.

Flexibility

The unique way each of us holds to his or her values is also a factor to consider as we seek balance in our homes. Some of us have very rigid views of right and wrong, and we're willing to die for our cause! Problems can arise when the people we're married to

> Whoever said it first spoke with insight and wisdom: You don't own children, you only borrow them.
>
> ANNE LINN

see the same issues from several different angles and don't agree that our choice is the only right one any sane person could make. Narrow or broad, black and white or gray, many couples see the issues of life in different ways. If they insist on their own way, they build walls to defend their perspective and pull out the guns to blast the other into submission. Some issues (probably fewer than the rigid people admit but perhaps more than the loose people want to believe) are crystal clear. Many, though, can be a little cloudy. And certainly, the ways we implement even the clearest decisions can take many different routes.

What's going on in your mind right now? If you're offended by my assertion that not everything is black and white, cut and dried, you're probably leaning a bit too far in that direction. Or if your lip is curled as you think about your rigid, demanding husband, you might be on the loose side of life. The point is this: Learn to appreciate the other side. That will be hard, but it won't kill you!

Lifestyle factors also can be viewed as narrow or broad. When you have meals, what you eat, how you spend Saturdays, what you wear to church, and a million other choices can become sources of understanding or causes of conflict for couples. Nowhere do we see the issues of rigidity and flexibility more clearly than in parenting styles.

Kim grew up in a strict household, and she can't stand for anyone to put her in a box. To her, nothing is sacred, and everything can be changed. Her husband, James, also had very strict parents, but he values the stability it brought to him and his siblings. He loves order and clear expectations. Soon after their wedding day, their differences became a source of tension. She demanded her own way and defended her position as the only good and right way to live. He did the same thing. As you can imagine, Kim and James have had tremendous problems in parenting their two kids. Every decision became a power struggle between the parents, and the kids were often confused. Of course, misunderstanding and demands in this area created imbalance in the family's emotional bonding. One of the boys gravitated to mom, and the other to dad. Now the armed camps were taking recruits!

Common Ground

When we don't grasp the necessity of balancing the opposite poles of emotional bonding and flexibility in marriage, conflict is inevitable. Parenting is just one of the battlegrounds where the couple fights. In his research,

> The most important thing a father can do for his children is to love their mother, and the most important thing a mother can do for her children is to love their father.

Dr. Olson found that one pole actually facilitates the other if both are appreciated. For instance, when people feel isolated, they long for togetherness, and when a family becomes too rigidly scheduled, throwing the schedule away for a day and doing something creative adds a sense of adventure to the relationships.

Love, fun, and deep appreciation for one another, though, aren't possible without an understanding that differences are good and that finding balance brings joy to relationships. Even families with the greatest conflicts can find common ground if people are willing to see things from each other's point of view. Then, areas that once caused problems can become stepping-stones toward love and trust.

What are some things that suffer when couples don't find balance in emotional bonding and flexibility? They fight over things like these:

- each other's role as parents
- the role of their own parents in giving advice, fixing problems, and shaping expectations
- who disciplines the children
- how discipline is carried out
- roles in doing housework, especially at different stages of the children's development
- how they respond when a child whines or demands his way

- schedules for meals, homework, play, and everything else
- how much to push the children to excel, and when to back off

In a study of parenting styles, John Gottman identified four distinct types of parents. Each of these relates in a unique way to emotional bonding and flexibility.[3]

1. Dismissing parents. These parents are too caught up in their own world of problems and opportunities to care much about their children's emotional health. They give lip service to their kids' emotions, but they would really rather not be bothered by them. They may see their children's emotional needs as threats or demands, so they discount them ("He doesn't know why he's angry—he'll get over it") or minimize them ("Her fear is no big deal—it will pass").

> Children need love, especially when they do not deserve it.

2. Disapproving parents. Condemnation and criticism are powerful forces that some parents use to control their children's behavior. These parents allow only pleasant emotions in their children, and they harshly control any hint of unpleasant ones. Some children learn to disregard their disapproving parents' anger, but the vast majority of kids experience deep wounds from their parents' negative words and the looks on their parents' faces.

3. Laissez-faire parents. Some parents believe they should allow their kids to express any emotion at any time, but they offer little or no instruction about how to process emotions. They're not emotionally uninvolved; they care deeply, but they believe in their children's self-actualization: "Let it be."

4. Emotion-coaching parents. The most effective parents are those who coach but don't dominate or control their children's emotional lives. These parents value the full spectrum of feelings and help the children learn important lessons from all of them. Emotion-coaching parents validate their children's emotions and never tell the children how they *should* feel. As the children mature, these parents gradually turn more responsibility over to the children at age-appropriate stages. This way, the children grow in confidence and become healthy young adults

> Your children will become what you are; so be what you want them to be.
> DAVID BLY

who accept responsibility for their feelings and behavior. Throughout the children's lives, the parents are the children's biggest cheerleaders. As the children become adults, the parents and children relate to one another as loved and respected peers, not as a parents and children any longer.

Our goal is not to find a balance of these parenting styles. All of us want to be emotion-coaching parents. We need to recognize our current behavior and the model our parents provided for us. But we need to grow from there and become wise, loving, effective coaches for our kids. This is the key to their emotional and relational health. And the way they see us is often the way they learn to view God.

We can find common ground with our husbands when we genuinely understand the different ways we think about bonding and flexibility and appreciate each other's point of view. As long as we insist that we are right and they are wrong, we'll continue to fight each other instead of becoming partners in raising our children.

Tim and I have learned the hard way to become friends who work together to find a common solution in raising our kids instead of being adversaries who defend our own turf. It makes a huge difference. In the early chapters of Proverbs, Solomon tells us that for us to pursue wisdom is crucial. That's what this chapter is about. Seeking wisdom with all our hearts is essential for us as marriage partners and parents. God's wisdom opens doors not only so we can know Him better but also so we can have healthy relationships.

> Get wisdom, get understanding;
>   do not forget my words or swerve from them.
> Do not forsake wisdom, and she will protect you;
>   love her, and she will watch over you.
> Wisdom is supreme; therefore get wisdom.
>   Though it cost all you have, get understanding.
> Esteem her, and she will exalt you;
>   embrace her, and she will honor you.
> She will set a garland of grace on your head
>   and present you with a crown of splendor
> (Proverbs 4:5-9).

As you take steps toward understanding your husband and helping him understand you, remember that you aren't alone. God's Spirit will guide and strengthen you, and He'll give you wisdom for each step you take.

To maintain a joyful family requires much from both the parents and the children. Each member of the family has to become, in a special way, the servant of the others.

POPE JOHN PAUL II

What You Can Say to Him

Before you have a conversation with your husband about your parenting styles, take some time to think and pray about the need for balance between two different poles in bonding and flexibility. Ask yourself these questions:

1. Do you tend to lean toward separateness or togetherness in emotional bonding?

2. Which tendency does your husband seem to prefer?

3. How flexible are you about your values and lifestyle choices?

4. How flexible is your husband in these areas?

5. What are the benefits of your point of view in these areas?

6. What are the benefits of his point of view? (This is a difficult but important item to consider.)

Get over the idea that your perspective is right and his is wrong. Another study by Dr. Gottman shows that successful marriages aren't built on mutual agreement about everything, but on qualities of friendship and mutual respect. Couples who have different backgrounds, different values, and different lifestyles can nonetheless have strong and secure marriages if they learn to appreciate each other. Parenting is a reflection of the parents' relationship with each other. If one is weak, the other will suffer, but if the relationship is based on friendship and respect, they will figure out a way to be effective partners in parenting.[4]

Author and counselor Virginia Satir once observed that we don't need to be perfect parents to raise healthy children, but we need to be "good enough" parents. In other words, we don't need to beat ourselves up if we fail from time to time. Our children, though, need their parents to find balance and common ground about the most important issues of life. No, I'm not talking about individual issues and schedules. I'm talking about the big picture of loving each other in spite of our differences, affirming each other, and seeing the other side even when we disagree. Love covers a multitude of sins in every relationship, including marriage and parenting.

Seeing the strength of our husbands' viewpoint isn't easy, especially if we've fiercely defended our perspective for many years. If you have a hard time appreciating the other pole, don't be discouraged. Ask God for wisdom and help, and talk to someone who will help you see life from another point of view.

Even when you recognize the validity of the other pole, you probably won't readily embrace it as your own. I'm not suggesting that. You need to have your own beliefs and preferences, but you can also appreciate the fact that your husband's perspective has some redeeming qualities. Your goal isn't to give in, but to find balance. As you progress together as parents (and in every other aspect of life), you'll find yourself saying things like, "You know, your way worked better in that instance." A few experiences like that can pave the way to a wonderful, renewed relationship.

If you've been critical of the way your husband thinks about bonding and flexibility, ask God for His forgiveness and then ask your husband to forgive you too. Tell him you want to be his partner and not his adversary as you raise your kids. Explain what you've been learning about the need to find balance in your parenting styles. Tell him some specific things you're learning to appreciate about his perspectives on these topics, and explain that you're committed to stop being demanding or defensive when you disagree with him.

The conversation about balancing your differences is only the first of a lifetime of many more rich, meaningful talks, but in the early steps of the process, be ready for a rough moment or two. When you dismantle the walls and muzzle the guns you've used for a long time, you have to rebuild trust that has been broken or eroded by the conflict. Is it worth the effort? Oh yes, it surely is! Your love for one another will grow stronger as you understand and appreciate each other.

And when you change your attitude and become partners, your kids may not know what to do with the change! They will need some time to adjust. They have probably played you against each other, and if they're older, they probably became quite skilled at it. Talk to them openly and honestly, and show a united front with your husband. Give the children time and space to absorb the change. All of you will thrive in the new atmosphere of understanding, partnership, and love.

In the Word: Chapter Nine Application

I am amazed that parenting can be not only one of the most difficult tasks on earth but also the greatest blessing God could give a man and woman. The two most important titles I have are "Mrs. Timothy Clinton" and "Megan and Zach's mom." I am blessed. Moses, the human writer of Genesis, attests to this blessing when he says, "God *blessed* them and said to them, 'Be fruitful and increase in number; fill the earth and subdue it'" (Genesis 2:28). This is known as the Divine Commission.

As we have seen in this chapter, our different opinions about parenting styles can lead to conflict in our marriages. In this section, I want to go deeper into God's Word and take a look at His desire and plan for parenting.

Differences Aren't Evil

"God created man in his own image, in the image of God he created him; male and female he created them" (Genesis 1:27). From the beginning of time, God made two distinctive types of human beings—male and female. Differences aren't evil. In fact, as we saw earlier, the differences between a guy and girl can enhance their attraction to each other. Moses concludes Genesis 1 by reporting, "God saw all that he had made, and it was very good" (Genesis 1:31).

In Genesis 2, we see how God created woman.

> The LORD God said, "It is not good for the man to be alone. I will make a helper suitable for him"…So the LORD God caused the man to fall into a deep sleep; and while he was sleeping, he took one of the man's ribs and closed up the place with flesh. Then the LORD God made a woman from the rib he had taken out of the man, and he brought her to the man. The man said, "This is now bone of my bones

and flesh of my flesh; she shall be called 'woman,' for she
was taken out of man" (Genesis 2:18,21-23).

Distinctively different—created by a perfect God!

A helper is someone who gives assistance. God created Eve to help
Adam overcome loneliness—to work with him and complement him
with her own uniqueness. In addition, children are born from the
unique differences associated with maleness and femaleness. A baby
cannot be born without the seed of the male and the egg of the female.
One cannot exist without the other.

From these verses we can gather that the God-given differences
existing between a man and woman are not bad. They actually form
a beautiful testament to God's creativity! But the actions associated
with these differences can lead to conflict. Too many times we focus
on changing our men, forcing them to see the world through our eyes.
Instead, we need to become students of our husbands and attempt to
understand their point of view.

Common Ground

Mark 3:25 says, "If a house is divided against itself, that house cannot
stand." In this passage, a group of scribes from Jerusalem accused Jesus
of being possessed by demons while at the same time casting them out.
Jesus asked them to explain how He could be possessed by demons
and cast them out at the same time. Cleverly using the analogy that
a house or kingdom divided against itself cannot stand, He taught a
principle that can be applied to our lives today.

You must seek common ground with your husband when consid-
ering how to discipline and parent your children. To find a balance
between your differences, you must sit down and communicate with
each other. Talk about role expectations, discipline strategies, daily
routines, and the like. When a mom and dad are in agreement, they
provide a structure that children can respond positively to. The children

feel secure, and they trust that their parents know how to protect them.

Becoming an Emotion-Coaching Parent

We looked at four different parenting styles according to John Gottman—dismissing, disapproving, laissez-faire, and emotion-coaching. The most effective parents choose to coach rather than ignore or control their children's emotional lives. In order to be a good coach, you must learn to regulate and control your own emotions so you can then teach your child.

One of the most difficult emotions to regulate is anger. Solomon writes extensively in the book of Proverbs about the importance of learning to control anger.

- "A wise man fears the LORD and shuns evil, but a fool is hotheaded and reckless. A quick-tempered man does foolish things, and a crafty man is hated" (14:16-17).

- "A patient man has great understanding, but a quick-tempered man displays folly" (14:29).

- "Better a patient man than a warrior, a man who controls his temper than one who takes a city" (16:32).

James also refers to anger management. He writes, "My dear brothers, take note of this: Everyone should be quick to listen, slow to speak and slow to become angry, for man's anger does not bring about the righteous life that God desires" (James 1:19-20).

Anger is an outward expression of an inward condition. Underneath anger lies an unresolved issue that propels us to become angry and maybe even explode. Many times, our kids or our husbands witness or even receive our anger.

It's okay to be angry. Paul writes in Ephesians 4:26, "In your anger do not sin." You can be angry and learn to appropriately express your feelings in a positive way, or you can blow up, causing damage to everyone around you. The choice is yours.

Your children learn to express many other emotions as they mature. Find ways to praise them when they tell you they feel sad, hurt, happy, excited, or angry. When you sit down to read a book with your children, have them tell you what the characters in the book might be feeling. Coach them so they can use their words to appropriately express what's going on inside.

Always remember, if you want to validate your children's feelings and help them learn to express themselves positively, you must first set the example. Proverbs 20:7 says, "The righteous man leads a blameless life; blessed are his children after him."

Reflection Questions

1. Are you and your husband on common ground when it comes to parenting your children? If not, when can you initiate a conversation to discuss your differences?

2. What is your current parenting style? If you are not an emotion-coaching parent, what steps can you take to become one? List the areas that need improvement.

3. Take time right now to pray for your husband and for your children. Then write an encouraging note or letter to each of them, expressing your desire to become his or her cheerleader for life!

I'm not telling him about...

10 My Hopes for the Future

Live with intention. Walk to the edge. Listen hard. Practice wellness. Play with abandon. Laugh. Choose with no regret. Appreciate your friends. Continue to learn. Do what you love. Live as if this is all there is.

MARY ANNE RADMACHER

A STUDY CONDUCTED BY the Clare Boothe Luce Policy Institute asked women about their daydreams. They replied with delicious thoughts of instant relief.

- 44 percent imagine winning the lottery,
- 43 percent envision a time with absolutely no stress in their lives, and similarly,
- 42 percent dream of being rich.[1]

What Women Want

I don't think the Clare Boothe Luce Policy Institute survey revealed what we women really hope to get out of life. Yes, it's fun to think about how our lives would change if we won tens of millions of dollars and sailed around

> What women want: to be loved, to be listened to, to be desired, to be respected, to be needed, to be trusted, and sometimes, just to be held. What men want: tickets for the World Series.
>
> DAVE BARRY

the world (or could buy gorgeous jewelry or spend it on whatever we want), but those are just passing fancies. What we really want—what captures our hearts and enflames our hopes more than anything in the world—is to be deeply connected to the men who are supposed to love us.

In an article for *Christianity Today*, sociologist Brad Wilcox reported the findings of his study, "What's Love Got to Do with It? Equality, Equity, Commitment, and Women's Marital Quality." At the end of his extensive research of a wide range of factors that promise to give us fulfillment, he made this conclusion:

> The biggest predictor of women's happiness is their husband's emotional engagement. The extent to which he is affectionate, to which he is empathetic, to which he is basically tuned in to his wife—this is the most important factor in predicting the wife's happiness. This basically drowns out every other factor in our models...We have to recognize that for the average American marriage, it matters a lot more whether the husband is emotionally in tune with his wife than whether he's doing, say, half the dishes or half the laundry. If the wife had to choose between having a husband who is taking half the housework and having a husband who is really making a conscious, deliberate effort

to focus emotionally on his wife, the emotional focus is much more likely to be a paramount concern.[2]

I know it's not politically correct to say that we need our men. Popular culture says that we're strong and independent and that we don't need anybody but ourselves. That may sound good to some audiences, but it doesn't ring true with most of the women I know. I'm not suggesting that we become doormats. Having arrived at the last chapter of this book, you know I don't recommend that at all. God wants us to be strong and independent but also to be engaged in meaningful relationships. We don't choose one or the other, but both.

Intimacy makes for oneness as well as healthy separateness. Our identity and our sense of security are determined to some degree by our talents and successes, but to an even greater extent by our connections with people. We look in the eyes of people we love and see a reflection of ourselves. We need people whose eyes tell us we're loved, accepted, and treasured. Their unconditional acceptance is our safe haven in the storms of life. Many people have already shaped our lives, but now, no one has more influence on our identity and security than our husbands—except Jesus Christ. God is our greatest source of comfort, peace, thrills, and joy. That's why I love the Scriptures so much—because God's love changes everything!

Snapshots

I've heard many young couples wistfully say, "We want to grow old together." But a few years later, inevitable tensions arise, and that statement might sound more like a curse than a blessing! At every point in our relationships, we hope to deepen our sense of belonging to one another. What does this look like? Listening is often the first thing people think of, but there's a lot more to it than that. Every couple finds their own way to express and experience closeness, but here are a few snapshots of genuine connections.

> All married couples should learn the art of battle as
> they should learn the art of making love. Good battle
> is objective and honest—never vicious or cruel. Good
> battle is healthy and constructive, and brings to a
> marriage the principle of equal partnership.
>
> ANN LANDERS

The Spark Returns

We can easily become too tired and too busy to relate in meaningful ways. We drag through some days just trying to cope, without an ounce of romance. But coexistence isn't what we're looking for! We long for the old spark of passion to ignite our love again. We don't need it to flame every minute of every day the way it did on our honeymoon, but once in a while would be wonderful.

Adventure

Get some adventure back in your relationships. Even those of us who live at the pole of tradition and established expectations want a little spontaneity from time to time, and women who thrive on the unknown need a lot of creativity in their relationships. We don't want to get stuck in a rut, complaining that change is too much trouble, but we don't have to be on the next space shuttle either. Grab your man and go for a picnic. Throw a toothbrush in a bag and drive into the mountains to find a little bed and breakfast for the weekend. You don't have to spend much money to bring some zest back into your marriage. If you have a hard time thinking of things, brainstorm with your friends, or better, with your husband.

Laugh More, Love More

Theodor Geisel, better known as Dr. Seuss, observed, "I like nonsense; it wakes up the brain cells. Fantasy is a necessary ingredient in living. It's a way of looking at life through the wrong end of a telescope. Which is what I do, and that enables you to laugh at life's realities." And on the other end of the literary spectrum, American psychologist and philosopher William James remarked, "We don't laugh because we're happy—we're happy because we laugh."

> A loving relationship is one in which the loved one is free to be himself—to laugh with me, but never at me; to cry with me, but never because of me; to love life, to love himself, to love being loved. Such a relationship is based upon freedom and can never grow in a jealous heart.
>
> LEO F. BUSCAGLIA

I have heard that kids smile 45 times and have 7 belly laughs every hour! When was the last time you laughed this hard? We can get so worried about money and bothered about the children that our minds become consumed with difficulties. We can't make all those things go away (though we may be able to make better choices about all of them). We can, however, learn to see the glass as half full. Even in dark times, and maybe especially in times of struggle, we need a generous measure of humor to lighten our load. Couples who find humor in their lives relieve a lot of tension and find common ground far more easily than those who see every moment as a threat. Laughing from time to time makes it much easier to lower our defenses and express the love that's sometimes buried by all our worries. Instead of complaining, tell stories. Instead of withdrawing, look for funny things to communicate. But be sure to never ever make your man the butt of your humor. That's not funny to him!

True Friendship

At the heart of romance is friendship. Friends look beyond their own interests and genuinely care about the things others care about. Great marriages are based on this single issue. Regardless of how many compatibility factors match up, and regardless of how much money a couple has, the single most important factor in bringing joy and security to a marriage is true friendship. Far too often, couples live separate lives. Over time, they drift apart, and eventually, they end up tolerating each other instead of loving each other.

> To the world you may be just one person, but to one person you may be the world.
>
> BRANDI SNYDER

Remember that great relationships find balance between separateness and closeness and between traditional expectations and spontaneity. One woman said that what she's looking for in a man is "my best girlfriend in a man's body." If that's what we're looking for, ladies, we'll never be happy with our men!

Value him for who he is, and build a friendship based on balance, not on his conformity to your values and perspectives. You married him because you respected him. Learn to respect him again. It's the foundation of a wonderful friendship.

Feeling Understood

When couples don't connect with each other, all kinds of doubts and fears fill their minds. One of the most important goals of any relationship is for both people to feel understood—not just to understand the other, but to actually feel that the partner really gets it.

Misunderstanding makes some people aggressive, but it causes others to withdraw behind walls of isolation. Each insight into the other person takes a brick off the wall and turns the guns away. And ladies, we sometimes aren't as perceptive about our men as we think we are. Sure, we think they're easy to read, but sometimes more is hidden beneath the veneer than we know, and sometimes our perceptions are clouded by our fears. We do well to add a touch of humility and wonder to our listening and understanding.

Stages of Hope

As we grow older together, our hopes change a bit. When we're young adults, closeness means the world to us. No amount of money and no level of success can fill the hole in our hearts—only love can do that. In those years, we need to devote our energies to the most important relationship in our lives. If we focus our hearts on tangible things and climbing the corporate or social ladder, we'll suffer twin pains: the fear of commitment and the fear of isolation. We won't know whom to trust, but we long to trust somebody. But if we learn to give and receive love, we'll reap the benefits of intimacy for the rest of our lives.

When we have children, we invest our hearts together in our kids. Some of us say that we didn't realize how selfish we were until we were married, but we saw our self-absorption in a whole new way when we had children! Oh, we love them dearly, but they required us to put ourselves aside all day every day. In the crucible of raising children, marriages can become severely strained—or they can become closer than ever before. Our hope in these years is to not be taken for granted, to not feel alone in all our responsibilities, to be honest, to not look like our mothers!

When a couple joins together in the task of raising children, they have a profound impact on each other and the children they raise. If they don't learn to communicate clearly and use the struggles to draw closer, the stress can produce tremendous tension in the relationship. Or they can become intimate partners who see the legacy of their love as their children grow to be healthy, happy adults.

And yes, many couples do grow old together. When their nest is empty, they face new challenges. For some, raising children provided the only glue in the relationship. When the children are gone, nothing is left. But couples that have learned the art of friendship grow deeper during these years. They see their purpose and legacy become a reality, and they feel deeply fulfilled.

Our hope isn't just to survive the stages of life. Our hope is in God. All of us experience struggles in each of these stages, and some of us feel as if we've blown it so badly that all hope is gone. I have good news— God can redeem any situation and bring hope to every heart! No, He won't turn back the clock and change history, but in His wonderful grace, He's willing to use even our biggest mistakes and blackest sins as colors on a new canvas of hope and love. We don't have to remain stuck in our painful past; we can learn lessons from those pains and move forward into the future.

New Patterns

> A married man should forget his mistakes; no use two people remembering the same thing.
> DUANE DEWEL

We may not feel that we have totally ruined our lives, but many of us realize our relationship with our men could use an adjustment or two. Let hope propel you to take action. Don't let the relationship drift any longer. Take stock of what's going on and the path it's taking, and then do something about it.

Many of the women I know insist that their men take the first step (and every other step) to build their relationship. That would be nice, but when it doesn't happen, these women get really frustrated. Then, instead of creating an atmosphere of love and understanding, they become more demanding or withdrawn. Not a pretty picture. We can be demanding and resent-ful, or we can take steps to create new patterns in the relationship. The choice is ours.

Old patterns are stubborn. We may detest them, but we may also be frightened of change—even change for the better. Change doesn't happen only because we wish it into existence, but still, the first step is to change the way we think. In this chapter, you might have been thinking, *Yeah, that's all very good for you, Julie, but you don't know my husband. Nothing works with him!* As long as you think that way, nothing will.

We need a God-sized vision of our relationship so we see our men and our future through His eyes. I'm not suggesting that when we pray, God will magically zap him into Prince Charming. Or a toad for that matter. No, God begins by working on our hearts and in our minds to give us a fresh perspective. We need a strong blend of hope and an understanding of the process we will engage in to get where God wants us to go. Gratitude and affirmation are the key ingredi-ents in any relational change. Start there and work on your own heart and thoughts first.

When our vision becomes clearer, we need a plan of action. If we've tried things before that haven't worked, maybe this time we should try something else, or try it in a different way (such as with a differ-ent tone of voice or a different look in our eyes). Don't demand that he change; make changes in yourself. Do you think he'll notice? I'm sure he will.

Romans 12:19-21 provides a template for our plans. Paul gives a number of clear directions about how to treat people, including the men we love:

1. *Love must be sincere.* We can't fake respect and affirmation. Our men may not be the most perceptive people on earth, but they can smell a fake a mile away. Don't say anything until and unless you mean it, and then say it with all your heart. If you have a history of creating distance or making demands, he may take a while to believe you, but don't give up. Love is persistent.

2. Honor one another above yourselves. Men thrive on feeling honored. Words and actions that affirm their efforts and show appreciation for what's in their hearts make them feel ten feet tall. And when we honor them, they instinctively want to show us how much they love us. Secondhand compliments are the most powerful. Sing his praises to your friends. When the word gets back to him, he'll feel tremendously honored.

3. Be joyful in hope, patient in affliction, faithful in prayer. It takes two people to make a relationship, but it only takes one to begin changing the atmosphere of a home. Unless our men are sociopaths, they should respond very positively to us when we are hopeful, pleasant, and patient. Think back over the communication you've had with your husband in the past few days. How much of it was negative (complaining, nagging, critical, or depressing), how much of it was affirming and positive (thankful, complimentary, or hopeful), and how much was distant (passive or withdrawn)? Psychologists tell us that twenty positive messages are required to overcome the impact of one negative one. How's your ratio? Do you need to change the equation?

Finding patience and praying for the men we love is a lot easier when our hearts and our words communicate grace. Hope is a powerful force in relationships. Without it, we give up quickly—on our men and on God. But with a strong sense of hope for the future, we persevere through difficult moments, and we trust God to work deeply in us and in our men.

4. Bless those who persecute you; bless and do not curse. Let's face it—when we don't feel loved and treasured, we easily get our feelings hurt. We hate it when we feel ignored, ridiculed, or taken for granted. It may not be persecution, but it sure feels like it! But when we turn things upside down by blessing our men instead of blasting them, the environment can change rapidly. How do we bless them? By speaking those words of affirmation we've mentioned. Even when our men are being difficult? Yes, especially when they're being difficult.

5. Rejoice with those who rejoice; mourn with those who mourn. I've talked to men who told me, "I just wish my wife would stop trying to fix me. When I'm angry about something, I wish she'd just say, 'That stinks. I'm so sorry that happened.'" Some of us feel threatened by our men's discouragement and anger, and we want them to feel better *now* so we'll feel safe again. In other words, when we try to fix their feelings, we're doing it for us, not for them.

Loving our men includes entering their worlds and affirming their perceptions and feelings. If they are happy about playing a good round at the golf course or closing a deal at work, we can rejoice with them. And if they are angry or disappointed about something in their world, we need to get under the rock with them instead of sitting on it by telling them they shouldn't feel the way they do. Emotional affirmation is just as important for him as it is for you.

6. *If it is possible, as far as it depends on you, live at peace with everyone.* As long as we're above ground, we'll experience disagreements and heartaches. The more intimate and vulnerable the relationship, the more we risk being hurt. Some of us are like porcupines that stick anyone who comes close. Those we love learn to be on guard whenever they're around us. Some of us are like volcanoes that are ready to explode without warning, and some of us are like butterflies hidden in a cocoon of protection. None of these approaches promote real peace. We find peace in relationships when we value open communication, respect each other's perspectives, and remain committed to resolve any conflict between us. Peace comes only when love replaces resentment.

7. *Do not take revenge, my friends.* One of the most significant ways we can change the atmosphere of a relationship is to practice the art of forgiveness. When we're offended, everything in us cries out for revenge, but God wants us to forgive the offender. When we choose to forgive, we're not saying the pain doesn't matter or that we invite the person to hurt us again. Rather, we're saying that we value God's way of grace over the natural reaction of payback.

Many couples are caught in a destructive game of hurt and revenge, chalking up grievances and trying to make the other person pay for what he's done. If you and your husband or boyfriend are doing that, stop. Trust God to work His goodness and grace deep into your own heart, and then make the courageous choice to forgive. Actor Peter Ustinov once remarked, "Love is an act of endless forgiveness, a tender look which becomes a habit."

Hope for the future is a powerful force for good in a relationship. Our hope isn't some ethereal, magical wish upon a star. Our hope is first in God and His good purposes for our lives, and then in the process of building (and restoring) relationships with the men we love. The truth is that no man can meet the deepest longing of a woman's heart. Only one thing can do that—a personal relationship with God through Jesus Christ. This kind of hope requires insight and courage, and it produces incredible results.

What You Can Say to Him

Distance and demands poison men's minds. Some men believe that all we care about is the money they bring home and the work they do around the house. The first thing to tell them, then, is this: "My real hopes aren't about houses, cars, jewelry, vacations, liposuction, or anything else we can see. My real hope for the rest of our lives is for you and me to enjoy each other to the fullest."

> There is nothing nobler or more admirable than when two people who see eye to eye keep house as man and wife, confounding their enemies and delighting their friends.
>
> HOMER

Talk to your husband about how the difficulties of life have caused you to drift apart or have drawn you together. And listen as he shares his perceptions of the impact those struggles have had on your relationship.

Tell him that you want the spark to return and that you're committed to balance, not to getting your own way. Take time to point out the things you're thankful for—about him, about his heart, and about how you've found love and life in your relationship with him.

Explain to him that you're committed to the adventure of life together. You may grow old together, but you never want to get into a rut. You might even say, "Be ready. I may surprise you!" He'll be ready, I'm sure. Paint a picture of what the future may hold for the two of you as you progress through the stages of life. Throughout this conversation and a thousand like it from now on, be thankful, be creative, and be hopeful.

If you've read through this book before talking to your husband or boyfriend about the topics of these chapters, you might feel overwhelmed by all the things you need to talk about. Don't panic, but don't give up. Pick one issue that is most important, and start there. Several conversations may be necessary before you make much progress. Change, especially in relationships, doesn't happen overnight. Communicate with grace and truth, and give him time to process the information you share. When you feel as if you've made progress in that area of the relationship, move on to the second item on your list. English poet Joseph Addison observed, "The greatest sweetener of human life is friendship. To raise this to the highest pitch of enjoyment is a secret which but few discover." I hope you are among the few.

In the Word: Chapter Ten Application

I want to close our time together by walking with you through one of the most delightful and instructive passages I have found in the entire Bible. Every time I come to it, God reveals something new and exciting. Paul included it in his first letter to the church at Thessalonica as part of his concluding exhortations:

> Be joyful always; pray continually; give thanks in all circumstances, for this is God's will for you in Christ Jesus. Do not put out the Spirit's fire; do not treat prophecies with contempt. Test everything. Hold on to the good. Avoid every kind of evil. May God himself, the God of peace, sanctify you through and through. May your whole spirit, soul and body be kept blameless at the coming of our Lord Jesus Christ. The one who calls you is faithful and he will do it (1 Thessalonians 5:16-24).

I used to be an elementary school teacher, and in case you haven't guessed already, I love organization. I am always thinking about how to package and present things in the best way possible to assist the learning process. A great way to organize and study this section of Scripture is to divide out and apply these instructions according to the promises of God. Then consider both the positive and negative instructions to you and your walk as a Christian.

Part 1. Notice the revelation and promises of God to assist His children in accomplishing these great tasks:

- God will reveal His will for your life personally—you no longer have to be confused about God's will for your life or live in fear because you can't see or hear Him.

- God will sanctify you completely so that you are holy and mature, lacking nothing.

- God will preserve your entire self blameless in spirit, soul, and body. (On resurrection day, God will raise you up whole and complete and invite you personally into His eternal kingdom.)

- God is faithful and will bring this all about based on His good promises, not on your performance.

Part 2. Notice the instructions to the church—to you and me as fellow Christians:

Positives—Do It	Negatives—Avoid It
Rejoice always.	Do not quench the Spirit.
Pray without ceasing.	Do not despise prophecies.
In everything give thanks.	Abstain from every form of evil.
Test all things.	
Hold fast to what is good.	

(It is important to remember that Paul is addressing the entire church with these spiritual commands—not just one individual.)

When I dwell on God's promises and His love toward me, everything changes. I end up praising and worshipping Him for who He is, for His faithfulness to me, and for His promises that extend to my husband and family. I am reminded that no one is like Him, and no one else is worthy of my worship and dedication.

When I dwell on Him, I am able to go forward and do the things He calls me to do—things that in my own strength are impossible to accomplish. Therefore, getting the order straight is critical—God first, and everything else follows thereafter.

Best of all, He calls us to let ourselves off the performance hook—to get out of His way and let Him accomplish what He promised. He will do what we are incapable of doing. Imagine that! His promise to redeem and perfect us is based on His character. He is the one and only God of creation and redemption, who will make us whole, complete, and perfect. And we will live with Him forever!

What if we spent 30 minutes every day taking our eyes off this broken world and instead fixing our eyes on God and His heavenly promises? What would happen? Think about that for a moment. I know in the span of 30 days or sooner, our lives and relationships would be transformed! We would have new, clean lenses with which to view the men in our lives, and we would love them the way God intended.

Let this verse inspire you today to take joy in the gift you have been given through Christ:

> This is how God showed his love among us: He sent his one and only Son into the world that we might live through him. This is love: not that we loved God, but that he loved us and sent his Son as an atoning sacrifice for our sins. Dear friends, since God so loved us, we also ought to love one another. No one has ever seen God; but if we love one another, God lives in us and his love is made complete in us (1 John 4:9-11).

We were born sinners, yet Christ died in our place and became the ultimate sacrifice. God loved us so much that He made a way for us to live through His death on the cross—not only on this earth, but with Him eternally in heaven one day. Thank God for His gift of Jesus Christ today and always!

Join with me, and together let's live, love, and celebrate our faith in Him!

Life really is all about relationships—first our relationship with Him, and then our relationships with those we hold close. When we allow God to soak into our being, life is radically different. It's filled with hope, meaning, healing, and new life. I pray His radiant blessings over you and your relationships.

Reflection Questions

1. How are you doing in your relationships with others? With the man in your life? With God? Take a moment to rate the relationships in your life on a scale of one (very dysfunctional) to ten (healthy, vibrant, and strong). What can you do today to move closer to a ten in every relationship you rated?

2. Now take out a piece of paper and write out a plan of action. Make three columns. Label one "personal." The second one is for the man you love. And the third one is for your children. Now write out your personal dreams and goals in life. Where do you see yourself? Your man? Your children? Start with a one-year goal for each column, and then write five- and ten-year goals in each column as well. Begin creating a plan of action that describes how you are going to meet these goals. I've heard people say time and again, "If you aim at nothing, you will hit it every time!"

3. Finally, do the same thing for your relationship with Jesus. What kind of a difference are you going to make in this world for Christ? Are you going to let go of everything you've been holding back and give it over to Him? Are you ready to live with your eyes focused solely on eternal things (2 Corinthians 4:16-18)?

4. Confess, commit, and change! Move forward from this day a new woman in complete freedom—free to be real in every area of your life and the relationships you hold dear to your heart!

Notes

Chapter 1—My Frustrations About Him

1. Dan Allender, *The Healing Path* (Colorado Springs: Waterbrook Press, 1999), 5-6.

Chapter 2—My Fears About Money and Security

1. Cited in Jonathan Leake, "Wealthy men give women more orgasms," *Sunday Times* (London), January 18, 2009. Available online at www.timesonline.co.uk/tol/news/uk/science/article5537017.ece.

2. Jay McDonald, "Gender spender: Sex sets your money DNA," Bankrate.com. Available online at www.bankrate.com/brm/news/sav/20000620.asp?caret.

3. Quoted in Martha Irvine, "A generation obsessed with having more stuff," *Houston Chronicle*, January 23, 2007.

4. National Endowment for Financial Education, "Motivating Americans to Develop Constructive Financial Behaviors," 2004, p. 7.

5. Jim Munchbach, *Make Your Money Count* (Friendswood, Texas: Baxter Press, 2007), 31-41.

6. Joe Lee and Thomas Parrish, "Dazed and in debt in the credit card maze," *Houston Chronicle*, January 21, 2007.

7. Elisabeth Elliott, *Keep a Quiet Heart* (Grand Rapids: Revell, 2004), 38-39.

8. Os Guinness, *The Call* (Nashville: Word Publishing, 1998), 4.

9. Ken Blanchard and Truett Cathy, *The Generosity Factor* (Grand Rapids: Zondervan, 2002).

10. Luci Shaw with Dallas Willard, "Spiritual Disciplines in a Postmodern World," *Radix*, vol. 27, no. 2. Available online at www.dwillard.org/articles/artview.asp?artid=56.

11. Brian Tracy, *Goals!* (San Francisco: Berrett-Koehler, 2003), 50.

12. Jay MacDonald, "Remarrying? Say 'I won't' to money mistakes," Bankrate.com. Available online at www.bankrate.com/brm/news/sav/20000118.asp.

13. June Hunt, *Counseling Through Your Bible Handbook* (Eugene, OR: Harvest House, 2008), 176.

Chapter 3—How I Want to Be Loved

1. Rodney Battles, "What Women Notice," *Nights in Atlanta,* March 18, 2009. Available online at nightsinatlanta.com/article/Women_Notice.htm.
2. Shaunti Feldhahn, "Your Love Is Not Enough: Why Your Respect Means More to Him Than Even Your Affection," *In Touch,* May 2005, 14.
3. John Gottman, *Why Marriages Succeed or Fail* (New York: Fireside, 1994).

Chapter 4—How I Feel About Our Sex Life

1. "What You Are Really Doing in Bed," *Redbook,* n.d. Available online at www .redbookmag.com/love-sex/advice/what-you-are-ll?click=main_sr.
2. "The sex-starved wife," *Redbook,* 2008. Available online at www.redbookmag .com/love-sex/advice/sex-starved-wife-5.
3. M. and L. McBurney, "Christian Sex Rules," *Christianity Today,* 2008. Available online at www.christianitytoday.com/mp/2001/spring/4.34.html?start=4.
4. "Married women hate sex," *MomLogic,* September 9, 2008. Available online at www.momlogic.com/2008/09/sexless_marriage_survey.php?page=2.
5. Susan Seliger and Cynthia Haines, "Why Women Lose Interest in Sex—and 10 Tips to Rekindle Desire," *Good Housekeeping.* Available online at www.good-housekeeping.com/family/marriage-sex/women-sexual-desire-0307.
6. "Size matters—new study delves between the sheets," LighterLife study, January 7, 2009. Available online at www.easier.com/view/Lifestyle/Relationships/Features/article-225059.html.
7. Shannon Ethridge, *The Sexually Confident Wife* (New York: Broadway Books, 2008), 112.

Chapter 5—My Past: Secrets and Private Issues

1. L.B. Finer and S.K. Henshaw, "Disparities in rates of unintended pregnancy in the United States, 1994 and 2001," *Perspectives on Sexual and Reproductive Health,* vol. 38, no. 2, 2006, 90-96.
2. David Reardon, *Aborted Women, Silent No More* (Acorn Books, 2002).
3. T.W. Smith, "American sexual behavior: Trends, socio-demographic differences, and risk behavior," *General Social Survey (GSS) Topical Report No. 25,* March 2006, 8.
4. John Piper, *Desiring God* (Sisters, OR: Multnomah Books, 1986), 250.

Chapter 6—How I Feel About Myself

1. Adapted from the American Psychological Association Task Force on the Sexualization of Girls, "Executive Summary," 2007. Available online at www.apa.org/pi/wpo/sexualizationsum.html.
2. An excerpt from Ellul's book is available online at jan.ucc.nau.edu/~jsa3/hum355/readings/ellul.htm.

Chapter 7—How He Hurts Me

1. Based on July 2005 U.S. Census.
2. American Bar Association, Commission on Domestic Violence: Survey of recent statistics. Available online at www.abanet.org/domviol/statistics.html.
3. T.W. Smith, "American sexual behavior: Trends, socio-demographic differences, and risk behavior," *General Social Survey (GSS) Topical Report*, no. 25, March 2006, 8.
4. R.C. Kessler, et al., "Prevalence, severity and comorbidity of 12-month DSM-IV disorders in the National Comorbidity Survey Replication," *Archives of General Psychiatry*, no. 62, 2008, 617-27.

Chapter 8—My Desires and Fantasies

1. Jeannie Kim, "11 'Don't tell the husband' secrets," *Redbook*. Available online at www.redbookmag.com/love-sex/advice/11-secrets-ll.
2. Courtney Mroch, "Fantasizing Wives," Families.com, May 1, 2008. Available online at marriage.families.com/blog/fantasizing-wives.
3. Ramona Richards, "Dirty Little Secret," *Today's Christian Woman*, September-October 2003, 58. Available online at www.christianitytoday.com/tcw/2003/sepoct/5.58.html?start=1.
4. Os Guinness, *The Call* (Nashville: Word Publishing, 1998), 4.

Chapter 9—How I Feel About Our Differing Parenting Styles

1. David H. Olson, et al, *Circumplex Model: Systemic Assessment and Treatment of Families* (Philadelphia: Haworth Press, 1989).
2. Cited in Froma Walsh, *Normal Family Processes*, 2nd ed. (New York: Guilford, 1993), 9.
3. John Gottman and Joan DeClaire, *Raising an Emotionally Intelligent Child* (New York: Fireside, 1997).
4. For more information about the study, and to take Dr. Gottman's "Relationship Quiz," visit www.gottman.com.

Chapter 10—My Hopes for the Future

1. Karlyn Bowman, "How Women See Themselves: The Latest Poles," Clare Boothe Luce Policy Institute, 2000. Available online at www.cblpi.org/resources/speech.cfm?ID=30.
2. Stan Guthrie, "What Married Women Want," *Christianity Today*, October 2006. Available online at www.christianitytoday.com/ct/2006/october/53.122.html.

Other Great Harvest House Books
by Julie Clinton...

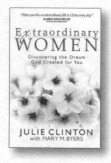

EXTRAORDINARY WOMEN

Julie shares biblical illustrations, life examples, and prayers throughout this book. You will learn to embrace extraordinary living when you discover God's dream for you, make every day count in surprising ways, and release control to take hold of God's freedom.

LIVING GOD'S DREAM FOR YOU

Julie shares devotions rich with wisdom gained through her ministry, life, marriage, and faith. Her message will inspire you to grab hold of God's dream for you as you discover the depth of Jesus' love, the wonder of your worth, and the joy of walking in His purpose.

To learn more about these books or
to read sample chapters, visit our website:
www.harvesthousepublishers.com

HARVEST HOUSE PUBLISHERS
EUGENE, OREGON